The Power to Speak Naked

How to Speak
with Confidence,
Communicate
Effectively, and Win
Your Audience

the

POWER

to speak naked

Sean Tyler Foley

NEW YORK

LONDON • NASHVILLE • MELBOURNE • VANCOUVER

The Power to Speak Naked

How to Speak with Confidence, Communicate Effectively, and Win
Your Audience

Published in New York, New York, by Morgan James Publishing. Morgan James is a
trademark of Morgan James, LLC. www.MorganJamesPublishing.com

ISBN 9781631954450 paperback
ISBN 9781631954467 eBook
Library of Congress Control Number: 2020950834

Cover Design by:
Lorraine Shulba
www.bluebugstudios.com

Interior Design by:
Christopher Kirk
www.GFSstudio.com

Morgan James is a proud partner of Habitat for Humanity Peninsula
and Greater Williamsburg. Partners in building since 2006.

Get involved today! Visit
MorganJamesPublishing.com/giving-back

Dedication

To my daughter:
May you always have the courage to speak up
for what you believe in, and the confidence
that your voice will be heard.

Table of Contents

Acknowledgments

This book would not have been possible without the support of hundreds of people, and unfortunately, there isn't enough room to mention everyone by name.

First, thank you to my wife for your never-ending support through the good times and the hard times. My mother, who has been awesome and incredible to me for many reasons. Your love and support are unparalleled, and I appreciate everything you have done and continue to do for me.

I also want to acknowledge everyone involved in Achievement Club, as well as all my elementary school teachers including Mrs. Neilson, Mrs. McGuigan, Ms. Young, Mr. Lobe, Mr. Irvine, and Mr. Turner. All of you have had a profound impact on my life, guided me through difficult times early on, set me on a path for speaking, and helped me find my voice in the world.

Also, I want to thank George Stone, Erin Wiebe, and Jim Senft, as you were instrumental in getting me on stage.

Thanks also to my Uncle Bob and Uncle Brian. You both have provided more mentorship, resources, time, love, and dedication than I could ever repay in ten lifetimes. I would not be the person I am today if not for you.

Thank you to the fantastic team of editors at Get You Visible for assisting with the refinement of my message, the remarkable efforts of Allissa Blondin at Beyond Transcription and Brian K. Wright at Success Profiles Magazine for their assistance with compiling the manuscript, the talented Lorraine Shulba for helping me visually represent my message, and the amazing team at Morgan James Publishing for helping me get my book to those who need the message within its pages.

This book is the accumulation of the love and dedication that I have received from many friends and family throughout my life who have helped me on the path to being on stage and becoming the man that I am today. I could not possibly thank you all enough.

Foreword

Have you ever dreamed of being on stage and speaking to a primed and eager audience excited to receive your content? Or maybe you are like the millions of people around the world who are terrified to speak. Either way, you have a story to tell and people need to hear it.

I have had the good fortune to work with some of the industry's top professionals including Brian Tracy, Robert Allen, Jay Abraham, Harry Pickens, and T. Harv Eker as an event planner and coordinator. I have seen what it takes to excel as a public speaker. Whether you are speaking in front of hundreds of people or a smaller audience, your ability to engage your listeners and connect with them is essential. The ability to win your audience in this way comes from speaking with confidence and communicating effectively.

The Power to Speak Naked will teach you the skills you need to make that happen. If you want to speak in public but don't know how Sean Tyler will teach you how to prepare yourself, engage your audience, and connect with a group of any size.

Sean Tyler addresses the technical aspects of public speaking like how to prepare a room, how to engage your audience before and during your talk and how to re-engage the audience when necessary. If you have to speak in public but don't want to, Sean Tyler will teach you how to overcome the fear of public speaking, so you can speak your truth in a powerful and authentic manner. In this book he leads you through mental techniques to calm your nerves, helps you break through your mental barriers, so you understand your fears and can get past them, and takes you through proven industry methods of preparing yourself to speak so you can deliver your message with confidence.

As a member of my Speak and Grow Rich Founders Circle, I have had many talks with Sean Tyler and have come to understand what drives him. He believes that everyone has a story to tell and with the courage and the tools to stand up and tell it, that story could impact millions of people around the world. Those who can truly master the art of public speaking and capitalize on the opportunities that it creates have one factor in common: They enrich the lives of their audience. This book will show you the secrets gathered over Sean Tyler's 30 year speaking career and his collaboration with hundreds of professional speakers and presenters on precisely how to connect with your audience and provide them with impactful and memorable presentations.

Everyone needs this book in their toolkit. Whether you dream of having a career as a speaker, or recognize that without developing your ability to public speak you will not reach your full potential in your chosen career, the simple solutions presented in this book will help you master your body and mind on stage so that you can captivate and engage your audience so that you can truly serve them. No matter what career path you have chosen or why you want to speak, anyone looking to grow professionally or personally will benefit from reading The Power to Speak Naked. Sean Tyler, as a speaker your confidence is contagious, and you have inspired audiences to know and believe that anything is possible. This book will empower so many people to tell their own story. Thank you for sharing it with us.

Gail Kingsbury,
Author of *Speak and Grow Rich:*
The Revised Updated version

Introduction

I still remember the first time that I had an impact with the spoken word.

I was at a regional speech competition delivering a poem called The Dragon, and there was a very emotional subcontext. In the poem, the dragon lived out his life and eventually passed away, and I remember being very moved by the subject. While I was performing on the day of the competition, I made two of the five judges cry. In that moment, I remember realizing not only the impact of the spoken word, but the power that I had in using the spoken word to influence others.

It was a very poignant realization for me to know that it's a skill that most people don't have. It's something that a lot of people struggle with, yet it comes very naturally to me.

At this point in my life, it is now my mission to help people use their voice to have an impact and share the messages that they need to put out there.

I believe that everyone has been uniquely gifted to share an important message with the world, and my passion is helping people discover that message and get it to their audience. It doesn't matter if that person is speaking to an audience of twenty or fewer, or if their audience is two thousand or more. If you are living and breathing, I am convinced that there is a reason and a purpose for your life.

You may have noticed that the title of this book is The Power to Speak Naked. If you are taking that literally, you might be a little disappointed because that isn't what this book is about—although what you do on your time is none of my business and I don't judge.

Instead, this book is about helping you find your authentic voice and share your passion with the world. We will explore a lot of different topics, such as how to prepare for a talk in terms of research, knowing your audience, the mental game, the delivery of your talk, and so much more. The nakedness I talk about here is the raw naked truth. It is about shining without hiding behind a facade and being who you authentically are.

If speaking in front of an audience scares you, this book will help you deal with that feeling of dread. Speaking in front of an audience is the thing that people fear the most—even more than death. However, as with anything in life, the more you do something, the easier it gets. Anything worth doing well is worth doing badly at first. I didn't pop out of the womb speaking to thousands of people, and neither did you. It's a skill that can be learned, and I am here to help you along the way.

If you follow the ideas and steps in this book, and I am confident that you will be further along in your speaking journey than you are right now.

Even if you are a seasoned speaker, you will likely find things here that you hadn't thought of before. I learn something new all the time when I speak. New situations and scenarios pop up. There is no way to plan for every contingency. If you are waiting for the 'perfect' situation, the 'perfect' audience, or the 'perfect' anything, you will be waiting a long time. The only way to truly learn a brand new skill is to practice.

I'm here to give you tools you need to be comfortable on stage and make an impact as a speaker.

Are you ready to begin? Turn the page and let's get started.

Your Opportunities as a Speaker

Whether you have ever given a speech or not, the opportunities for personal growth and career enhancement are enormous in the current marketplace. If you aspire to speak full-time, you may find yourself in a lucrative career as well.

How big is the potential for you as a speaker?

Whether you are looking to grow your speaking business, or perhaps simply using the power of speaking to build your clientele, there's no question that finding and monetizing the right opportunities can be difficult. However, it's usually because there are some common mistakes that speakers and business owners make that they may be unaware of.

Whether you are a business owner, coach, or speaker, one of the most profitable things that you can do is to speak on more stages. It shortens any sales cycle as it gives your audience the chance to get to know, buy from, and view you as the authority that you already are in your field.

Any time you are required to speak or give a presentation, you are selling. You may not be selling a physical product, but you are selling an idea, a belief, and, most importantly, *you*—or perhaps all the above.

Learning to speak effectively and communicate your ideas efficiently is one of the greatest things you can do for personal and professional development. If you don't embrace speaking as part of your business model, it can hold you back from having an impact professionally, socially, or even financially.

A perfect example of this is my very good friend, Amanda.

Amanda didn't have just a fear, but a true phobia of public speaking. She realized that this phobia was limiting her in her career as a psychologist. She can speak one-on-one to people because that's an integral part of her business. However, the minute she must pitch herself on a bigger scale, she becomes terrified. She had an incredible vision to serve many more people in her business by creating remote access for her counseling services—but she couldn't find the courage to pitch the idea despite being very social, likable, smart, articulate, and physically stunning.

She was approached by a couple of event organizers about speaking at a conference, but she couldn't say yes. Her fear wouldn't allow her to take that step. Yet, her dream of expanding her company into an online on-demand counseling service was alive and well.

As a result of letting her fear control her in that moment, she realized she had missed an opportunity. She reached out and asked me to help her get over the fear of speaking. She knew that speaking had to become an important piece of the puzzle.

I worked with her very diligently for six months. We used a lot of techniques to get her past her comfort zone and onto the stage. To this day, she is still terrified to get on stage, but the difference is that she has pushed herself past the fear.

During this six-month period, she got in front of several investors and spoke at a couple of conferences. She was able to expand her business from a small private counseling practice with five to six clients to a thriving company.

She now has twenty counselors working for her, and she is flying around the country securing new contracts for her business. It's currently a multi-million-dollar empire. In the course of twenty-four months, she went from a small practice to what I just described. The transformation has been nothing short of phenomenal—and conquering her fear of public speaking and implementing the strategies around it made a huge difference.

Embracing speaking as a tool to build her business allowed Amanda to reach people who needed her but otherwise knew nothing about her or that this type of counseling resource was available. Amanda is changing lives because she has learned to overcome her fear of public speaking. The only thing that held her back from a multi-million-dollar business was adding speaking to her business model. She now has proven authority in her industry, and she can reach many more people than she could one-on-one. Everyone told Amanda that her vision for creating a remote, online, on-demand counseling service couldn't be done, but she believed in her vision. Speaking was the last piece that she needed to add to see it become a reality.

> Speaking in front of audiences could be the difference between surviving and thriving in your career.
> The sooner you embrace it, the faster you build credibility in your industry.

Where are the opportunities for you to incorporate speaking in your business or career?

First of all, if you are working for someone else and are in management or in an executive position, you will be required to speak to your team, whether it is a small group or for your entire company. In the U.S. alone, there are an estimated twenty-one- million people in such positions.

Next, if you are a salesperson, you will certainly be giving talks on a regular basis to potential customers either individually or to groups regarding the products and services you have to offer. An estimated fifteen-million people fall into this category.

In addition, if you are in network marketing, your business growth depends heavily on your ability to speak to individuals or groups about what you do. If you are one of the estimated five million people in this industry, this book is certainly for you.

Also, if you are an entrepreneur, your ability to make a persuasive presentation will determine if you will make a sale, get a loan or line of credit for your business, get a preferred deal from a supplier or vendor, or a whole host of other scenarios which directly impact the growth of your business.

If you are active in a non-profit organization, giving a successful talk can impact not only the donation levels your organization receives but the goodwill of your community too.

Clearly, the opportunities are nearly unlimited for you to learn and grow as you embrace speaking as part of your normal routine. Just remember, learning to speak in front of groups can not only be lucrative but life-changing; not only for yourself but for the market you serve.

If the thought of speaking on stage is terrifying, that's OK because you are not alone. This book will guide you through some ideas and strategies that can help you in your journey. Even if you are a pro at this, I often find that even one new idea can add a huge impact and make a difference.

With that in mind, in the next chapter, we will talk about some of the things you should consider before your talk once an opportunity to speak is presented to you.

Key Takeaways: ————————————

- The potential to exponentially grow your business can depend on your willingness to embrace public speaking as a means to generate clients.
- No matter what industry you are in, there is an opportunity to use speaking to build authority, generate leads, raise donations or capital, or be seen as a leader—all of which have the ability to help your career.
- If speaking scares you, keep reading. I will discuss ideas and strategies which can help you overcome your fear.

Wait, Who Am I Talking To?

Knowing your audience is critical to an effective presentation. I routinely tell my clients that while they don't have to have expert knowledge of their audience, they should know enough to relate to them.

You should know enough to reference their interests, their mission, or their leadership if, for example, you're speaking to a trade association or union. You should have some remarks relating to your specific audience that demonstrate you are not just showing up to speak, but that you considered the perspective of who is in front of you.

If you need to, contact your host and ask questions about the group. They might appreciate that you want to do some customization for your talk. You might learn about an important member of the organization who will be in the audience and can be singled out for podium praise; perhaps there is a charity that has benefited from the group's work—and that's always a good point to mention. The bottom line: do your homework.

> Know some characteristics about your audience in advance. It will give your audience the feeling that you have prepared for your talk and have taken an interest in them.

Your answers to the questions to the checklist below should help you conduct effective research. Depending on your subject, some of these questions will have more value than others. If you're unable to answer a particular question, or if it isn't relevant to your situation, skip it. You may also think of questions unique to your situation which may be more appropriate for your needs.

Keep in mind that the primary purpose of this analysis is to help you communicate effectively with the people who will be listening to your speech.

Here is the checklist:

1. **Audience size**

   The size of your audience is important for several reasons. If your group is very small, the need for microphones and other audio/visual equipment would be minimized. A smaller group might also mean a less formal event. That doesn't mean you should take the event less seriously, but it does mean that everyone should be a lot more relaxed. A smaller group would be easier to know in advance, especially if you have a chance to mingle a little bit before your presentation (or event) starts.

2. **Demographics**

   Knowing the demographic make-up of your audience can be helpful. For instance, are you speaking to mostly men? Mostly women? What is the age range? Are they college educated or not? If your talk is political in any way, knowing which way your audience leans can make a difference in how your message will be received. You want to make sure your topic is not over everyone's head, nor do you want to insult audience members' intelligence by unnecessarily spelling everything out if they are familiar with your topic.

3. **Cultural considerations**

   This relates to the previous point about demographics of your audience. If you are speaking in a foreign country, for example, you would be well advised to find out if there are significant cultural differences to consider. For instance, speaking in the United

States or Canada might be much different than presenting in a Middle Eastern or South American country. Certain words might mean something entirely different in one country than they would in another. The time of year could also be a factor as various types of holidays are observed in diverse parts of the world at different times. As always, do your homework in advance.

4. **Audience expertise**

This will depend greatly upon the type of event you are speaking at. Is this an industry event? If so, a certain level of expertise from your audience will be expected. If this is a breakout session or a mastermind event, that expertise could be somewhat higher. However, if this is a general event, or if you are speaking in a contest situation, your audience may know very little about the topic. Also, if your presentation is on a new or immerging topic, your audience could be looking forward to what you know because they may not have much prior knowledge.

5. **Authority and trust**

If you are well-known or have written a book, this problem begins to solve itself. If you have neither of these things going for you, then you can still prove credibility in your talk if you have solved a problem that your audience might be facing. It gives you a reason to briefly describe that moment or mention it in passing during your talk. Many speakers may prove expertise by mentioning credentials, but people care a lot more about the results that you have generated for others. If you can prove that, you are well on your way to solving any perceived credibility issues.

6. **Misconceptions about your subject area**
This question is crucial if your topic is either new or controversial in any way. If your topic is new, ask yourself what questions someone may have, then work hard to address those within your presentation. If your topic is controversial, acknowledge both sides of the issue and have *plenty* of evidence to support your side. If some audience members hold the opposite view that you hold, don't necessarily expect to change their lifelong opinions in one speech. Logic alone will not always win the day. Emotional appeals and specific stories (case studies) can be very impactful. Knowing the demographics of the audience, of course, will help.

7. **Interest level in your subject**
If you are speaking at an industry-related event, this should be self-evident. If you are speaking in a more general setting, then you should make the effort to justify your topic to your audience. What is

in it for them, and why do they *need* to be informed about your topic?

8. **Timing/duration**

   The length of your talk will depend on the type of event you are speaking at, and perhaps the time of day. If you are the last speaker of the day, or if you are speaking at the end of a multi-day event, your audience might be tired. If the speakers ahead of you went over their allotted time limit, you might need to adjust and speak for a shorter length of time. However, in no case should you go over your allotted time. If your talk is engaging and entertaining, your audience won't mind how long it is, but if you are B-O-R-I-N-G, your audience may give you a much shorter leash.

9. **Format**

   This also depends on the type of event you are speaking at. Is it an evening event, or an all-day affair? Perhaps you are speaking at a multi-day conference, or maybe you are speaking at a hands-on style workshop. The type of event will go a long way toward guiding the format of your talk. Therefore, having an ability to customize and tailor your talk to each situation is critical. It gives you the chance to 'save the day' and be memorable, not only to your audience, but to the organizers as well.

10. **Audience familiarity with you as a speaker**

    Your audience will need to learn a little about your background if they don't know you, and they will want to ensure that you are qualified to speak to them about your topic. If your topic is not well-known, then, of course, more background information will be needed. No matter what, your audience should be familiar with you and your topic by the time you finish your talk.

11. **Objective**

    This depends a lot on the goal of your talk. If it is a workshop style presentation, then your agenda is to teach and be authoritative. If your presentation is a TED-style talk, then your goal is to present ideas that stimulate thought and advance ideas for people to incorporate into their lives. As a result, your agenda or desired result has much to do with the goal of the talk as well as the environment of your presentation.

12. **Desired outcome**

    Knowing your desired outcome is critical, so when planning your talk, begin with the end in mind. Think about taking a vacation in your car. You could pack the car and start driving down the road, but if you have no idea where you want to finish, you leave too much to chance. Your talk should have a specific destination in mind. What do you want your audience members to learn or do because of your presentation? You need to guide them in the direction you want them to go.

Clearly, knowing your audience, your topic, and the environment of your presentation are all crucial to the success of your talk. You can ask the event coordinator for the information that you need and, in many cases, the answers to your questions may also be found online. If you know speakers who have presented at that event before, their feedback may be invaluable. Also, if you know previous attendees, this may be a great source of research info as well.

The more you know, the better your chances of having an effective and impactful presentation. Don't be afraid to go the extra mile. You want to be remembered for the right reasons. The more prepared you are, the more your event planner will appreciate you. This could improve your chances of being invited back next time.

Key Takeaways: ——————————————————

- Having a clear idea of who your audience will be is critical to the success of your presentation.

- Use the checklist in this chapter to guide your preparation for your talk. If you have any questions about the nature of the talk you are going to give, ask the event planner or the person who invited you.

- Be clear about the desired outcome of your presentation. Will you be educating or asking the audience to do something? Will you be allowed to sell anything or issue a call to action? Know this beforehand and respect the wishes of the person who invited you.

The 5 P's - Plan, Prepare, Practice, Present, and Participate

Now that you know who you are speaking to, it's time to get ready for your talk. Clearly, you won't simply walk on to a stage. There is a process that you will need to follow to get yourself ready for the occasion.

This process is commonly referred to as the five P's.

The five P's have been around for a long time. I got these from speaking in 4H (an international youth development group) when I was a kid, so if some of this sounds familiar to you, it's because I've adapted a lot of this from my public speaking experience with 4H as a child and now as a judge of their regional speech competitions. This is a great framework to work through when putting your talk together. The last thing you want to do when being asked to speak is to 'wing it'. While *speaking naked* is about being authentic, there is a difference between being 'real' and being 'unorganized'. Clearly, one is far better than the other.

Let's explore this framework in detail.

Plan

Surprisingly, the planning step is either ignored or poorly executed by a lot of people who have a message to communicate. The following is a tale of two clients, one who gets it right and the other who doesn't. You will figure out quickly which one did a better job of planning their message.

I host a radio show called *The Entrepreneur Speaker's Corner*; it's a one-minute segment on a local radio station. It's a paid advertising spot for people to come on the show and deliver a pitch. As part of their fee, they get a half-hour coaching session with me to prepare them for the show. The people who take advantage of that always shine.

Recently, I finished working with a client who paid for a spot but didn't show up on time and didn't take advantage of the coaching. By the time the client arrived, we had only ten minutes to get this done from start to finish. He paid very good money to do this advertisement. However, I knew it wouldn't get him any business, and the way he sounded might repel people from working with him if the program aired.

As you can imagine, it was a disaster. In fact, none of the takes we did were usable. I ended up reaching out to him and offering to do it again.

On the same show, I had another client who was very set in how she wanted her story to be told—but it was too long. We have sixty seconds to work with, and factoring the intro and outro into the equation, there are only forty-five seconds available to get the message out. She utilized the training and paid for two more half-hour sessions to tailor her message to get it as effective as possible within the allotted time frame.

The producer sat in on some of the sessions, and he loved this client's message so much that they used her spot as a promo. The end result of this was that she took full advantage of the planning, paid for several sessions, worked hard to make the message amazing, and then got additional free exposure via the promo ads that continued to run on the station beyond her paid promotion.

How can this story relate to the speaking world?

Some people are content to step on to a stage or walk up to a podium and start speaking—essentially, they decide to 'wing it', or say whatever comes to their mind at that moment. In my experience in judging and evaluating speakers, the majority of speakers who attempt to do this go down in flames—just like the first client discussed earlier—because they may only have a general idea of what they want to say, or perhaps no idea at all.

> Plan your talk in advance. The audience will be able to tell if you are trying to 'wing it' or not.

Therefore, the first thing you have as a speaker is a clear topic of discussion. A presentation is not meant to be a *Seinfeld* episode— no-one wants to hear a speaker go on and on about nothing. If you are speaking at a conference, the parameters of your topic will be defined, at least to some degree. But if you are speaking to a Toastmasters group, for example, you could talk about anything you want. But you must decide what that will be.

Once your topic is solidified, it's best to envision your presentation with the end in mind. You want to come up with a plan because, as the old adage says, "If you fail to plan, you plan to fail." When you envision your talk with the end in mind, then by definition there must be an outcome you want your audience to have. What is that outcome? What takeaways do you want audience members to have? Is there a call to action? What do you want them to do or think when you are done?

Planning also means considering who your audience members are. That could make a big difference in the types of words you use in your talk, as well as how deeply you need to explain your topic.

Finally, you will need to select an appropriate title for your talk. It needs to be compelling enough to grab not only the audience's attention, but the event planner's attention as well because in many cases you will be selected (at least in part) because they feel you're the right speaker for the job. Think of the title for your talk as a click bait news headline. The goal of the title is to reach out and grab some-one's attention hard enough that the response is, "I *have* to hear this person speak."

As a speaker, you want to set yourself up for success. Planning is very important, all the way from selecting your topic to the actual content in your presentation. The content will depend greatly on the length of time you are given to speak. If you have five minutes, you are going to have to be very succinct with your words, and what you're saying in your message must have an immediate impact. If you have fifty minutes, maybe you have more time to explore what you're discussing.

Again, consider who your audience is. Who are you speaking to, and what is their level of understanding of the topic that you're discussing? Where is the talk taking place? Are you presenting in an auditorium? Is it going to be a lecture style? Are you speaking in a classroom setting?

What are the dynamics of your presentation? Will you require the use of technology during your talk? I know speakers who love PowerPoint—I'm not one of them—but the direction of your talk will be affected by whether or not you will need any kind of A/V gear to help facilitate your presentation.

Practically speaking, what are some tools you can use to plan your message?

Brain mapping is a great way to do this. Simply use recipe cards or index cards to write down individual ideas. This allows the flexibility to shuffle the cards and put your thoughts in whatever order you need to make the message flow better.

Another great planning tool is an audience questionnaire. There is a template that I typically use to gather as much information about the audience prior to my talk, and it is posted on my website. You can access the site using the QR code at the beginning of the last chapter the QR code below so that so you can see what types of information I try to obtain prior to my talks.

On the site you can also access my complete speech planning template to help you plan your talk and make the experience as smooth as possible.

For a sample speaker planning checklist, visit seantylerfoley.com anytime or use the QR code here. Clearly, planning is very important to your overall success. Let's look at what else is important.

Preparation

Once you've chosen your title, you've got your audience in mind, and you made plans concerning your presentation, you're ready to prepare the talk. Planning is your Coles Notes bullet point version, so preparation is organizing what we're going to speak about. If it's prepared, it will be more interesting to the audience because there is thought and connection behind it. Fail to plan, plan to fail.

When you're developing your talk, your audience will feel and react according to your level of content and preparation. Lots of speakers think, "I can speak off the hip," but everybody will know if you're unprepared. You can tell when somebody is faking it and haven't put any prep time into their speeches. You inertly and instinctively feel it in your gut.

One way that you can prepare for your talk is to test your material during a short Facebook Live. Get some feedback about the content of your talk in advance. This will encourage you to be even more prepared. In fact, it is common for comedians to test their material as they continue to refine their routines. They keep what works and discard what doesn't. The principle is the same for you as a speaker. Find out what resonates with your potential audience—and what doesn't—and prepare accordingly. If you like, you can also hashtag #thepowertospeaknaked so I can give you feedback.

Preparing doesn't have to be difficult. It simply means that your talk needs a basic structure in place. Here are some things to consider:

- Introduction: Why did you choose this topic? Why should the audience listen?
- Body: Present your topic in an organized manner
- Summary: Review major points of discussion

When you prepare your talk, you're going to want to have the audience in mind. Therefore, I like to start with the end of the presentation. I like to know how I'm going to close because that is the very last thing that people remember. Now, you can stumble in the beginning but still find ways to bring your audience back. In the middle, you can also lose people and still get them back, but your ending must close in a powerful way.

Whether you're trying to leave an impact or make a sale, you need to bring your talk to your main point or takeaway for your audience right at the end. If you haven't planned the conclusion of your talk and don't have a good solid finish, a couple of things happen. You lose the message, and you'll lose the impact, and a lot of us—myself included— will ramble unnecessarily because we don't have a solid, pre-defined endpoint.

That's why I plan my end first. Once I know how I'm going to end, then I structure the beginning. With an introduction, consider some question marks to check off in your head. Why did you choose that topic? Did you select that topic, or were you 'voluntold' you needed to speak on it? Why should the audience listen to you? That is a great way to start.

Here is an example: "My name's Sean Tyler Foley. I am the author of *The Power to Speak Naked*. The reason I'm presenting this training to you because I do a lot of public speaking."

It's that simple. It's giving that credibility up front because the audience then has a reason to listen. Sometimes that's going to be done in a synopsis or introduction for you, but even so, the people who are promoting it don't necessarily know who you are. Having that prepared synopsis is a great way of letting your audience know why they should listen to you. They may have some initial prep, but then again, they may not. They may not know who you are until you show up on stage. Work a brief synopsis of your credentials in at the beginning and let the audience know who you are and why you're qualified to speak to them. It can be very brief, and it doesn't need to sound like you're bragging.

Good preparation also means researching your topic thoroughly. Brian Tracy has a great philosophy about this topic, and it gets to the point. If you don't have twenty words for each item or subject you're going to talk about, you're not an expert yet, so do a little bit more research. You need to be able to talk on the fly and, if necessary, you need to be able to fill that time. The best thing you can do for yourself is research your topic. Have stories, examples, and references to give your presentation some depth. If you are dealing with an audience where people may think that they already "know it all," having specific stories unique to you can be a great way to keep things interesting. You don't have to go overboard with your research, but I'm one of those people who really does like to over-research and cover my bases because you never know when you're going to get an oddball question from your audience.

If you get a question that you can't answer, one of the best things you can do is acknowledge that you don't know the answer. I'm going to get more in-depth about this later, but if you get stumped and you just don't know, don't make stuff up. Acknowledge that it's a good question and that you're not a subject matter expert in that one particular area because your focus is here in *your* area of expertise. Then you can pivot back to where your strengths are. If you are well-prepared and you've done good research, you're able to say, "That actually isn't my area of expertise, but what I have been focusing in on is this area," and you get your credibility back right away. That all comes with the preparation, so research is a key consideration in this whole process.

As an example, audiences love quotes. A good friend of mine and amazing speaker, Jared Morrison, knows thousands of quotes because he is so well read. He pulls them into his presentations all the time. Some other brilliant speakers who I have shared the stage with and who use quotes with effortless ease are Les Brown and Mark Groves. If you ever get a chance to watch them speak publicly, they can pull quotes from thin air in a manner that seems as effortless as a rabit from a magicians hat. They are always on topic and audience appropriate because they are all very well read, and they do a lot of research on the topics that they present. Bottom line, research is key for presentations to be effective.

> Research is the key for presentations to be effective.

Sometimes you need to have graphics or charts to make your main ideas clearer. I don't like PowerPoint, but I do like to be able to draw charts or pictograms to illustrate points. Personally, I like flip charts. I prepare them ahead of time so that I have them in my preferred sequence and can flip each page over as needed. Having a flip chart allows me to use pictures, charts, and graphs when I do need to illustrate a point, and it allows me freedom and flexibility to create on the fly if something comes up during the presentation that I was not originally prepared to cover.

If you feel that you absolutely cannot present your topic with your voice alone and you need visuals to go with it, then take the time to prepare those—as long as they enhance your message.

It is so important to make sure your visuals, whether flip charts, PowerPoint, or props, support what you are saying. Don't create charts or PowerPoint slides with the idea of reading your whole presentation. It is boring for your audience because, at that point, you may as well have handed them a worksheet to read, and it's a sure sign that you are truly unprepared. Simply use PowerPoint or other visual as a prompt for your talk.

Pro-Tip: If you are going to use PowerPoint, use pictures more than words whenever possible because pictures communicate more than words do. I suggest using a maximum of five slides. PowerPoint slides should be used to support your talk, not be your talk.

If you use text in your PowerPoint slides, use short sentences of three to five words. If you use bullet points, use three at the most.

You don't want to clutter your presentation, so ideally, use one bullet point and one image per slide. Also, avoid putting your slides on a timer. You want to spend as much or as little time on a specific slide as you need. If you rely too much on animation, fades, or dissolves with your slides, it looks more like a gimmick and will distract from your message.

I mentioned not writing down your speech on Power-Point slides. Even if you are not using visual aids, don't write your talk verbatim or try to remember it word for word when you are writing your presentation. When I'm preparing my talks, I have bullet points. Just use an out-line or list of points you want to discuss that you can refer back to if needed. When you are doing your prep work, try to keep that in mind because then you will have more of a flow, making your talk sound more natural. If people interject during your talk, it doesn't throw you off track knowing that you have an outline to follow.

One last thing about preparation: look your best. First impressions mean everything, and a bad first impres-sion is nearly impossible to overcome. Think about how you want to be perceived and dress accordingly.

By now, it should be clear that preparation is the key to making your talk effective.

Practice

Now you need to practice. The more you practice and the more you rehearse, the more comfortable you're going to be with your talk. Don't neglect this crucial action.

As an example, I had to do a monologue when I was fif-teen years old. It was the final presentation for a drama course that I was taking, and it accounted for 50 % of my grade. I figured I would do very well since I was a professional actor for nine years by that point and was in a couple of shows at that time. I'm not afraid to admit that my ego was massive back then. I memorized scripts overnight, so I was not concerned about my ability to pull the monologue off. As a result, I did no practicing. On the day of the performance, when the lights came on, I froze. I didn't have a clear idea of what I was supposed to say, so I simply improvised the whole thing. Needless to say, it was a complete disaster. To make matters worse, a couple of years later I was a teaching assistant for the drama instructor, and there was a student who was my direct competition for roles in the past—wouldn't you know, he did the same monologue, and he was brilliant. In fact, he ended up getting scouted and did some incredible things going forward. He went on to have a very good acting career. If I had done the prep work and practiced, I might have had a similar opportunity. My lack of preparation and practice for this performance was critical. People may say the other guy was "lucky" but, in reality, luck is when preparation meets opportunity. You can't be lucky without preparation and practice.

Hopefully, the lesson is crystal clear—practice.

When it is time for you to practice your talk, it's best to be in a place where you will not be disturbed.

You may be wondering where you can practice undisturbed. I like to practice in my car and my shower. As weird as it is, the shower gives good acoustics and allows me to 'hear myself'. The shower and driving also require some brain power, so it is a good test of how well I know my material if I can talk and perform another task at the same time.

The other reason I love practicing while driving as that I get to give a presentation to 10,000 commuters every day. They don't know that I'm talking to them. Someone watching from another vehicle would likely think I'm singing songs, but I'm not singing to the radio. I'm going through my talk and prepping for my next speaking gig. I'm simply saying my speech out loud. Sometimes I put my phone down on the side, and I record whatever things come up. This allows me to come up with ideas and have them documented for later.

There are so many opportunities for you to practice—in the shower, driving, doing laundry, vacuuming. Basically, any task or chore that requires some time and will divide your focus.

If you are a member of my coaching or training programs, you can send us a message, and we can help you out. Just turn on your webcam, let us know what you are working on, stand up in front of your camera, and either myself or one of the coaches will help you. The group is very supportive, so we can all get on a Zoom call and help you as you work out the mechanics of what you want to present. That is my promise and my guarantee to you. You can learn more about how to join the program at the end of the book.

Present

Now we get to present. Standing up and speaking for our audience is the Holy Grail, but at the same time, that's also the hardest part. If you are a speaker, then any chance you get to speak, whether someone needs a guest trainer or there's a need in your work environment, step up and say *yes*.

Let's say you're not doing this as a full-time gig yet and you still have your daytime job - if there is any chance to get up and give a speech, a presentation, or a PowerPoint, be the one to volunteer. I'll let you in on a secret. It's a fast way to accelerate your worth within your company if you're willing to speak because nobody else wants to. I know that's how I was always successful in the careers that I was in. When I was still in the corporate world working 9-5, the fact that I was always willing to take on a presentation or lead a discussion put me on a fast track to rise within the various organizations I worked for. They just knew "Tyler will do it." Having the courage to stand up and put yourself out there speaks volumes to your leadership and your confidence, and you will accelerate your career if you volunteer to present.

> If someone asks you to speak, say yes. You will be miles ahead of those who don't.

Another way to start presenting is with speaking competitions or groups. If you have a local speaking competition, get up and take part, even if it's simply reading a poem. That is how I got started in public speaking when I was six years old. I was in the theater, and I was rehearsing lines, and then when I didn't have a theater gig, I entered the regional, provincial, and national speech competitions. If there is a regional speech competition in your area, go out and sign up. Get that practice in and present something. I can't stress it enough—any chance you get, go out and talk. Watch other presenters so that you can see different styles. It will give you a good sense of the things that work and things you would change if you were presenting the same material. You can learn different tips and techniques. Even if you see a speaker who is struggling, it's a great learning opportunity as well to see why that person is having issues.

In addition, if you want to improve at public speaking, go do karaoke. That may sound counterintuitive, but karaoke is a thousand times harder than public speaking. With karaoke, everyone knows the lyrics because they are posted for all to see, and most people know the tune. If you make a mistake, the whole room will know. But if you are delivering a speech, no-one has your script, so nobody will know if you made a mistake or not. It's all about getting up in front of people, having fun, and being willing to be vulnerable.

Yet another way to get some practice is to join a Meetup group. I have one called Perfect Your Pitch that gives speakers an opportunity to practice what they are currently working on. If you can't find a group like this, then form your own speaker club. Get like-minded, or better yet,

Growth Minded people together who want to work on their public speaking in a supportive way. For me, starting my own speaking group was a great way to bring my clients together with an audience where everyone could practice.

Some speakers will be very experienced, whereas others will be novices and their speeches won't always go well in the beginning. If you see a speaker going off the rails, then show them support because at least they're trying.

At the end of the day, that speaker got up and delivered a presentation. That's why my wife and I binge-watch TED talks, and why I always agree to judge competitions when asked. Any chance you get to participate in public speaking, whether as a presenter or as an audience member, say yes. It all goes back to my point about preparation and doing your research. When you're doing your planning and your preparation, research is key.

If you watch some TED talks, it'll help you as a speaker on the technical side. It will also give ideas on what you want to speak on. In addition, TED talks often open your mind to new ideas and concepts and can help you start connecting these together. At the beginning of my journey, I learned a lot from my own speaking experiences, and I have adapted what I learned so that now I can put my own spin on these concepts. The best way to learn is to do, so get out and do some speaking.

If you are concerned about whether or not your talk will go well, keep in mind that knowing your material and practicing are critical. Do your presentation on your own with notes, then without notes, then in front of a friend, your family, or a classroom. Slowly graduate to a larger group to calm the nerves. All the while remember to breathe and have water nearby if needed. Time yourself so that you don't go over your allotted time limit.

Getting in front of an audience and doing the presentation is the key to getting better. Remember, your audience is rooting for you—and so am I.

Participation

The last P that we're going to talk about is participation. By participation, I mean both with participating in the talks and watching them.

Remember, we're delivering talks, but not because we love to hear ourselves speak. You need to find places not only where you can speak but also where you can take in other talks. Be a participant in this career and support it as a profession. When you're delivering a talk, remember it is not about you. It's about what you can give to your audience when you can. The more you can elicit participation from them, ask for questions, check in with them, and make sure that everybody is doing OK, the better.

Eliciting audience participation can help your presentation. If you can work in parts of your talk where you can connect with your audience, check in with them, and make sure that the points and the takeaways that you planned at the beginning are being absorbed by your audience, the better your talk will be perceived. After all, it's all about them, so we want their participation and input. Even doing something as simple as scanning the room to see if audience members are leaning forward in anticipation versus sitting back in their chairs and looking uninterested gives us a good gage as to how our message is being received. Being aware of their body language and what they're experiencing is essential.

In that planning and preparation stage, try to envision yourself as the audience member who is engaging in your talk; then elicit that participation because that is when you get power as a speaker (when you're able to really empathize with your audience and make them feel as though you are speaking directly to them individually). It all goes back to planning, preparing, and knowing who your audience is because it may be this demographic today and another demographic tomorrow. Therefore, you may need to switch up some of your key points and how that presentation comes together.

This is why I never memorize my talks. Instead, I'm memorizing key takeaways so that I can provide that information. This is what you need to do as well. The reason I do it is so that I have the freedom to be flexible, and the freedom to move and re-position things for my audience as needed. If I'm losing participants somehow, it gives me the opportunity to reconnect with them.

Sometimes telling a joke and mispronouncing words on purpose can be a good trick to reconnect. Even adding humor can be a great way to break any nervousness you might have and engage your audience at the same time.

How can we add humor? Two things: If you're not good with humor, don't attempt a joke. It can become awkward and weird. What works for me may not work for you. For example, I tend to make fun of myself in a self-deprecating way. As a result, humor always works for me. If you ever hear me present, I always point out about how I have nothing to complain about because I'm a white male from a middle-class family who is educated and doing what I love for a living, so where do I get to complain? Usually, the speaker before me has overcome some hugely adverse tragedy, and then the speaker after me is going to close with how they have overcome some hugely adverse tragedy. It almost always gets a laugh and allows me to ease tension in the room.

For some speakers, sarcasm can work as well. Sarcasm is a subgenre of humor. It works great if you're good at it and your audience knows and is comfortable with its use. I know because I use sarcasm all the time and it lands effectively probably 35 percent of the time. It needs to be laid on thick, and you need to be over the top. However, you need to be careful, particularly if you're speaking in the self-development world as a motivational or inspirational speaker. Words have meaning. Words have an impact. Sarcasm is usually going against the grain of the truth. Sometimes people take things literally and don't realize you are being sarcastic, so there is the potential for your message to be taken in the opposite way that you intended.

This can have an adverse effect on a talk, even if it's being done by someone well-known. I've heard some big-name speakers— six-figure speakers—who have said some horrible things under pressure and then they've had to turn around and apologize. No speech is going to be perfect, so be aware of how sarcasm can impact your message and your audience. Do I use it? Absolutely. But it needs to be a tool in the arsenal, not the tool in the arsenal. The biggest draw back to sarcasm is that it enforces the opposite message you are trying to convey.

For example, consider you're asking a multiple-choice question and you want your audience to pick the answer. Good practice is to have the correct answer reinforce the learning objective. A poor multiple- choice question, for example, could reinforce the negative.

For instance, if you present a multiple-choice question, you may ask, "Which of these is incorrect: The sky is blue, night time is dark, the sun is bright, or the mountains are small"? The answer is the last option, but it is reinforcing a negative or incorrect concept. The takeaway that your audience is left with is a statement with a false concept. You always want to construct a multiple-choice question where the correct answer is a positive reinforcement of the concept you are trying to illustrate. This is the draw back of sarcasm, and why it should be used sparingly.

Here are a couple of things that you can do. If you know you're funny, throw in a joke/sarcastic remark. Some people are naturally gifted at it, and humor comes naturally to them. An audience who is laughing is having a good time. If you can elicit emotion out of your audience, whether that's laughter, crying, or empathy, you get your audience on board with you anytime you can make them feel something, which means that you're doing a good job as a speaker. If you are funny, use it. If you're not funny, but you know that you want to use humor because you want to make an impact, then some reliance on visual aids is OK.

A lot of people I talk to think they are not funny. Any time someone tells me they are not funny I do the following exercise with them. If you are one of those people, try this: I want you to write down the last ten times you made somebody laugh, and I bet that you don't have to go back further than a week. This will help you realize that you can make people laugh. You just might not be a comedian. However, if you want to hone your comedic skills, go to an open mic night and be bold enough to participate. You will find out quickly what material works and what doesn't. I'll give you an example. I do a lot of safety training, and I talk about why communication is key to this industry and how to get the right message out. It's a dry topic, so there's a video that I play where two hunters are out walking in the woods, and the guy accidentally discharges his gun and shoots his buddy. He gets on the phone with 911, and he says, "Oh my God! Oh my God! I just shot Jimmy!!" Then the 911 operator says, "OK sir, calm down. I need you to make sure he's dead." The guy says, "OK, I can do that," and then all of a sudden you hear a bang. He shoots his buddy again, and he says, "Yeah, he's dead. Now what?" Everybody gets a chuckle out of it, and it breaks the monotony. The point is, if you're not funny, you don't necessarily have to be. The internet can also be a great help. When people send you chain jokes or memes that go around via email, use them. I worked with a speaker who wanted to do after-dinner speeches, and the first book he wrote was a compilation of memes and jokes. This guy charges $6,000 for after-dinner speeches, and he does corporate gigs. All he does is read the jokes out of his book, and then he gives the book away as a promotion. Genius. So, if you're not naturally funny on your own, don't worry about it. Find the things that make you laugh and that are relevant to your talk and use them.

This is where the planning, practice, preparation comes in. If it's relevant to your talk and you want to find something funny, Google 'funny', and then insert your topic slash video and you'll be golden provided that it is relevant and doesn't detract from your message.

Key Takeaways: ————————————

- Everyone gets nervous. The more public speaking you do, the less of an issue this will be, and you will gain self-confidence along the way.

- Picture your talk going well, and remember all the hard work you have put into your presentation beforehand.

- Remember the five P's: Plan, Prepare, Practice, Present, and Participate. If you remember to do all these, you will have a great experience on the stage. Do *all* these, don't skip any of them. Everyone must start somewhere, and once you get started you will want to speak again...and again...and again.

How to Engage and Re-Engage Your Audience

Picture this scenario for a moment.

You are on stage delivering a talk. You've planned, prepared, practiced, and now you are presenting to your audience. But as you look out at the crowd, you notice something disturbing.

You see evidence of the dreaded 'glazed over' look from your audience—the one where they're shifting, they're restless, they're not paying attention.

I have had this situation happen more than once—it happens to all of us.

Here is one such story and how I handled the situation. You might find this to be helpful.

Recently, I did a two-day facilitation about safety. It's a topic nobody gets excited about, but I have stories that make the topic interesting. On this particular occasion, I was speaking right after lunch, so I could tell early on that this group was not fully engaged. If you think about how you feel after eating a meal, you can probably understand it can take a while to get fully focused again. For this reason, I normally schedule an activity after lunch to break the normal pattern. However, the way this presentation had gone, we got to the activity before lunch, so I went into lecture mode after the meal because that was next on the agenda.

To further complicate things, I was having an off-day. I had some personal issues going on, and I was lost in my own thoughts. Consequently, I was not giving 100% to my audience, and I soon realized they weren't giving me 100% back either.

The combination of these resulted in an experience that I didn't feel particularly good about. Some people in the audience had their heads down; others had their eyes closed. I was getting empty looks, and some were even checking their cell phones. I felt tension in my body, and I was no longer speaking from my diaphragm, but was speaking from my head which resulted in a nasal sound quality. I started talking louder to try to keep their attention, and my pitch was in a higher register than normal. I was no longer communicating from a place of authority.

I knew I needed another chance to re-align, so I created an activity. I asked the audience to stand up and find someone new and review the biggest takeaways from the day so far. This accomplished a couple of things. It gave the audience members a chance to get up and move, and it gave me a chance to assess where I was. I took some deep breaths, got centered, and released my tension.

This energized everyone, and I was now centered and began speaking from a place of authority. I felt it in my voice and was now in command again. I had everyone's attention and the day went well from that point on.

If you ever find yourself in a similar situation, I want to share some tips and techniques you can use to re-engage your audience and to get them back before you lose them completely because it happens to the best of us. Once you start talking and people's minds start drifting, there are strategies to help you out.

John Medina, who is a psychologist and author of the book Brain Rules, found in a series of studies he did that the average attention span for any human being is ten minutes. If you want proof of that, watch cartoons. If you've ever watched Saturday morning cartoons, you will notice that they are typically organized in ten-minute blocks.

If you or anybody you know has kids who are watching cartoons on Netflix, you will notice that they have two short episodes per show. Typically, they are twenty-two minutes long, eleven minutes each, with a one-minute opening sequence, and there are usually three quick transition breaks. This is to keep kids' attention span going because otherwise—squirrel—their attention spans are gone. Knowing this, the problem with being in an audience is that this ten-minute window encourages an audience to tune out the majority of our senses. The audience's job is to typically sit there and listen, so we as speakers need to be able to break that pattern up, hopefully in ten-minute segments, to maximize attention. The strategies for re-engaging your audience are very similar to the ones you would use to engage your audience. You can use these strategies so that you don't lose them.

Be Engaged

If you're starting to lose your audience, you can do some things to bring them back, to grab their attention, and change up the pace of the presentation.

One of the first things that you can do is be engaged yourself. If you're not fully focused, why would your audience pay attention? You yourself need to be in the zone and in the mindset to be able to deliver a good presentation. The next thing that you can do is tell them what their takeaway is, so that you prep and prime them for what is to come.

Here is a great example of this.

There will be three takeaways here:

1. How to engage your audience.
2. How to bring them back if they disengage.

3. Finally, eight tips to reset that button to bring your audience back, to grab their attention.

So now the audience knows there will be strategies for engagement, re-engagement, and eight takeaway steps. Their brains are now primed.

Relate the Content to Your Audience

The next thing that you can do is tell a story within the first five to eight minutes, preferably one that is going to relate the content and material to them. That will help your audience have an emotional connection and a tie into it so that they are now primed. They're going to focus on you, so they do not automatically want to drift.

When I do safety presentations, I talk about the lessons I learned about safety while doing stunts in film and television. The title of my talk is, 'The Safest Job I Ever Had Was Jumping Out Of Windows'. When I go on stage, I intentionally do a pratfall because the number one cause of hospitalizations in North America is falling. It's also the number one reason why workers end up claiming Worker's Compensation or losing employment. Of course, the whole thing is a setup. I have a maintenance person mop the stage five minutes before I go on, but they don't put out the 'Wet Floor' sign. When I do my fall, it looks real, but then I stand up right away and assure the audience that I'm OK. Then I ask the audience to consider what might happen if they lost their ability to earn an income after an accident.

Then I talk about a previous injury I had where I hurt my back while picking up my daughter when she was six months old. I was in such pain that I couldn't work for two weeks, and I had to cancel some speaking gigs.

It certainly grabs attention.

You may not have a dramatic example like this to work with, but there are always ways to connect to your audience. For instance, if you're delivering data, make the data relatable. Or better yet, ask your audience what the numbers mean to them and either positively reinforce their input when correct, or reframe and provide context if their understanding is poor. Make sure to make the information relate to your audience. I mentioned earlier that the typical audience is going to lose its attention span within ten minutes. Well, how can I make that relate to you? I can tell you a personal story about how I've seen an audience drift off as I did earlier so that you can picture it happening and perhaps trigger your own memory of a similar event.

I do instruction, specifically adult education, for a good chunk of my business portfolio, and I deliver eight hours, sixteen hours, sometimes two-and-a-half or even ten-day training seminars. I've already mentioned that people can drift after eating, so the time of day of your talk is important to consider. That ten-minute chunk works great for the majority of the day, but if it's that hour period after lunch, you may need to shorten when you're changing up your cycles with some of the tips and tools I will present in this chapter.

If you are presenting right after lunch, you may need to shorten that ten minutes to a five to eight-minute window just to get people's attention. Your best strategy would be to tell a story within the first five to eight minutes as mentioned a bit ago. That story will sum up why they need to pay attention to you and will engage your audience right way.

The Four P's

Consider the four P's of the voice (not to be confused with the five P's of presentation discussed before): Pace, Pitch, Power, Pause. Let's quickly define these points:

Pace: This is the speed at which the speaker is talking.

Pitch: This refers to how high or low the speaker's voice is (high voice vs deep voice, for example).

Power: This refers to the intensity and forcefulness of the speaker's voice and should be used only to emphasize an impactful or important point.

Pause: This can be used strategically to allow the audience to digest something important that the speaker just said.

Use these four P's, get familiar with how and where they go in because by emphasizing specific words, changing up your pace, changing your tone, or bringing your audience in by telling them a secret nobody else knows, you instantly grab their attention because you've changed your delivery. The brain will have noticed a change. The audience will instantly lean forward because something is different, and the brain recognizes the difference. And then it starts paying attention because it wants to know why, and as soon as you can get the brain going, the crowd now has to pay attention to figure out what it is. Emphasize keywords when you're delivering a talk to achieve the same effect.

Warm-Up Exercises

Doing warm up exercises before your talk can be tremendously helpful. Just as singers need to warm up their voice before going on stage, so should you, as a speaker, do this.

Here are some quick examples of some exercises you can use, and you can do all of these for fifteen to thirty seconds each, or longer:

1. Stand up, raise your arms in the air, and take a deep breath. Loudly release your breath and drop your arms to your sides.
2. Warm up your lips. Say the word "ba" forcefully.
3. Vibrate your lips together like you are making a motorcycle noise, then buzz like a bee. Alternate back and forth between the two.
4. Warm up the tongue and say "la la la la la" in an exaggerated way with your mouth wide open.
5. Roll an "r" with your tongue.
6. Make a siren noise. Use the word "we" for the high pitches, and the word "oh" for the low pitches. Therefore, this exercise sounds like "Weeeeeee...ooohhhhh...weeeeeee...oooooooh".

For more exercises, use the QR code here to link to my website.

Use Humor

If you're comfortable with adding humor to your talk, do it. I discussed this in the last chapter, and it's a great way to break the pattern. If you can, interject humor within your talk and plan to add a joke every eight to ten minutes. A simple way to do this, whether you think you are funny or not, is if your presentation uses PowerPoint or some kind of presentation software; put in a meme or YouTube video that is relevant to your topic. Then you don't have to be funny yourself, but you can still throw in humor. This works well if you know that you are losing your audience. You can program your slide deck or your presentation so that it's automatic within the presentation. This will help re-engage your audience if they start to go in another zone.

Surprise Them

Another strategy to engage and re-engage an audience is to do something unexpected. Get loud, get quiet, walk off the stage. Those things can take an audience by surprise because it wouldn't have occurred to them in that moment, but now they're paying attention again. Other things you can do that are out of the ordinary include doing a magic trick, or even singing and dancing. You pick what's going to be comfortable for you, but do something unexpected. Attention comes back immediately. And when you're doing all these strategies, try to remember WIIFT (What's in it for them). Always remember your audience. You are there to serve them, not yourself, so these strategies need to be put in place to keep and maintain their attention so that you can provide them with value. As a caution, keep in the back of your mind that when you're using these devices, and don't overuse them. Also, don't use the same ones repeatedly because your audience will start to see the pattern and they will lose their effectiveness—this will ultimately mean that your audience is not getting the value from your talk.

Therefore, remembering 'What's in it for them?' is the best way to provide your audience value. Our goal is to give them something which will benefit them, but we must engage them for the message to be effective.

Create Energy

As you are reading this, I want to ask you, regarding engaging an audience, "What is a strategy that has worked for you or hasn't worked for you?" Now, see what I just did? I asked a question which demanded a response, which is a great way of engaging or re-engaging your audience and getting that interaction and participation.

By the way, if you're going to use this questioning strategy, demonstrate to your audience the desired response by putting your hand up high when you ask the question. By doing this, you engage your audience in a powerful way because they can easily raise their hand, but it requires their commitment. It's a way to get people to mirror what you're doing, so that's a terrific way to get engagement and interaction.

Tony Robbins does this incredibly effectively, and he pairs it with getting people to say something. So, don't just have your audience do a show of hands, but rather have them make a verbal acknowledgment as well. Some examples of other speakers who do this include Phil Town, Gerry Robert, Colin Sprake, and others who are well-known and very effective in what they do. If you ever get to see speakers like this, they will say something like, "If you're with me, raise your hand and say, 'Aye'."

You get the whole audience to do this several times in a row in order to reinforce the participation. For example, "If you're tired of doing this and you want to live this way, raise your hand and say AYE. If you know that you have more potential in you than you ever thought possible, raise your hand and say aye."

This is an incredibly effective way to get people ramped up and engaged. It creates energy, which then gives the speaker energy and gets the audience back on pace. When it comes to polling your audience, you can also ask a question such as, "On a scale of one to ten, how effective has this training been for you so far?" Raise your hand high as you ask these types of questions so that the audience will know that this is the response you want from them. As you do this, tell your audience to raise their hands high if they agree with what you are saying.

You might begin by saying, "On a scale of one to ten, raise your hands high..." and ask them to raise their hands with the number of fingers to answer your question. It changes things up. Remember, this is a way to actively engage your audience. They have to evaluate how they feel and what they are thinking. They aren't just passively sitting in their chairs.

Check in with your audience every five to eight minutes. Ask, "How has this resonated so far?" Assess if there are any questions from the audience. Ask if anybody experienced something similar to what you are talking about. If you get a yes, you can invite someone to briefly elaborate. It's a great way to check in with the audience. You have a mini Q and A, and then you can judge your time, and you've served your audience without having to wait to the end.

Use Less Time Than You Are Allotted

Here's a great pro-tip: always speak for less than the time allotted to you. If you're given thirty-five minutes, talk for twenty-five. It's a courtesy to the venue. You may be thinking, wait a minute— they paid me for thirty-five minutes. No, they paid you to be there for thirty-five minutes. They didn't necessarily pay you to talk for thirty-five minutes. I know that seems counterintuitive because you're a speaker, but if you are answering questions, you are still serving your audience.

Sometimes you might follow a speaker who went too long, and the event coordinator might appreciate that you are helping to bring things back on schedule by being a little shorter in your talk. The best way to serve your audience in that instance is to incorporate the questions and answers into the talk instead of waiting until the end. It's an excellent strategy to serve your audience better because they're able to engage with you and get their questions answered quickly.

Think about it like this: if you attend a lecture and have a sudden, brilliant thought but don't write it down, you run the risk of not getting to ask your question, or you might even forget what it was. Why? Because the top speaker went on and on and on, and then when it was time for questions, you realize that you had thirty brilliant ideas, but now you don't remember what they were. You didn't write it down because that speaker was so engaging that you didn't want to look down and start writing notes. So, allowing for a little time for a Q & A is an excellent way to serve your audience better and break up the pace.

Get the Audience Actively Involved

You can serve your audience better by letting them know they should write down what you are about to say. If you have a powerful point to make, say, "Write this down." It's very directional, it helps you maintain control, and you are serving them by letting them know that they should make a note of what you are about to say.

This is an excellent way to create a pattern interrupt and re- engage the audience. The people who brought pens will, in fact, write down what you are about to say. The people who didn't bring pens will pay extra special attention because they want to remember what comes next. This strategy serves both whether they have a pen or not. So, tell your audience to. "Write this down," and then give them the information that you really need to emphasize to them. As you are progressing through your talk, keep in mind the four P's: Pace, Pause, Power, and Pitch. Learn them, know them, love them.

Some of the other ways that you can engage audiences, in addition to getting them to write things down, is to have them say something out loud. You can also do group exercises. You can have your audience members pair up with one another and have them take turns sharing experiences they've had that are similar to what is being discussed, or perhaps share their favorite takeaways so far with one another.

As soon as you get them to do that, it changes the pace, it breaks up the talk, and it gives you a break. It gives you a moment to recollect your thoughts, especially if you are losing your audience. That gives you that moment you might need. Use thirty or forty seconds to do the "turn to your neighbor" exercise, take a sip of water, collect your thoughts, and then bring them back with an audio cue or a movement.

Using some of those transition phrases is a great way of resetting because people know that one section is done and you're moving into another section.

John Medina observed that people will only remember the first thing and the last thing that you say. So again, those micro question and answer periods every five to eight minutes will be helpful for you because it breaks up your talk. If you talk for your full sixty minutes and you don't break it up, there are fifty-five minutes of content that your audience will lose. But if you break up a sixty-minute talk into ten-minute segments, they remember the beginning and the end. So now you have six sections, which means you have twelve takeaways that they're going to pull from your talk. It's a good strategy, so try it out and see how it works for you.

One more thing you can do with your audience is to have them stand up, move around, and talk to a neighbor. Do an exercise with your audience. A good friend of mine, Jason Krause, does a lecture called The Science of Success. He discusses how mind connections and neurons work, and how high-performance people think. He is a former Olympic athlete, so he is a well- qualified source on this topic. One of his strategies is to pair people up and have them introduce themselves to each other. One person talks for thirty seconds and the other person talks for the thirty seconds, and he cues them.

Everybody's shaking hands and introducing themselves for thirty seconds apiece, so they shake hands for a minute. He does this exercise three times, and he will have them ask their partner about their first car, their first job, the time when they've gotten into the most trouble, or whatever topic they can think of. The cool thing about this is he gets everybody moving because they have to stand up. They also have to physically interact with somebody. It's a great way to break up the presentation, and then he teaches the exercise as a point about connection and how we engage with the audience.

Use Visual Aids

Another thing you can do is to have visual aids in your presentation. They can prime your audience to look for or to pay attention to something. This will refocus their minds. If you have visuals on stage, you could ask, "As you look at this, what part of this image impacts you the most?" You could draw the audience to their favorite color, for example, or you could ask what stands out most about what they see. Having them physically think about what they are seeing will actively engage their senses. If you are doing a sales pitch, ask which stat stands out the most to them. They don't need to share it out loud, but now everybody feels that they've become personally involved in it, even though everybody will have a different answer.

Be Inclusive

Another great way to engage everybody is to use "you" and "your" because you are essentially speaking to individual people, even though you're speaking to an entire audience. This will also help engage and/or re-engage your audience. It's a strategy known as inclusive framing. If you want to speak to grow your business, you should be familiar with this concept. For example, you could ask, "Who here has played an instrument or who has ever wanted to play an instrument?" If you ask who has played an instrument, you're isolating people who have done so. But asking who has ever wanted to play an instrument, is much more inclusive. This broadens the range of people included in your discussion. So "who is wanting to" is a broader inclusive frame, whereas "who has" starts to narrow your effective audience to that particular niche.

Finding those inclusive statements, anything that changes the tone of the room and gets them to interact with you or other audience members, will change the room dynamic and engage the audience even more.

Use Transition Phrases

Other examples of engaging and re-engaging phrases you can use include: "What I'd like to ask you to do now...,"

"What I want you to take away from this is...," "The thought I'd like to leave you with is..." and so forth. These are all really good phrases to break out and transition in your talk because it makes people think. If you want to see further examples, do this fun little exercise. Go back throughout this chapter and make a note of how many times I use inclusive statements and phrases, such as "you" and "your", and the transition phrases I used.

Figure out places where you would have inserted some more of those transition phrases to break up the pace, as well as some of these techniques to re-engage a live audience within your own talk or presentation. Another thing that you can do that is super effective if you feel you are losing your audience is to acknowledge the fact. You can say, "I can feel the energy in the room, and maybe I am starting to lose people." What have you accomplished by saying this? You have broken the pattern and changed up the pace. You have asked the audience for engagement and participation. They also have to acknowledge that they are no longer actively engaged in what's going on. So, it works very effectively.

If you have injected humor, and the joke falls flat, you can do what one of my favorite speakers, Gerry Robert, does. If he tells a joke and he doesn't get the laugh, he will turn to the audience and say, "Oh, come on now. That was funny…just a little laugh?" And he will get a little laugh out of it. He plays on the failure, and it forces people to laugh—maybe not a full-hearted belly laugh, but they do laugh. Acknowledging the feeling in the room is a great strategy. Acknowledge the failure, and that unto itself can sometimes bring people back.

Key Takeaways: ————————————————

- First and foremost, in order to engage or re-engage your audience, you yourself have to be engaged. You have to be in the zone so that mental prep ahead of time will go a far way in making sure that you don't lose your audience. Prevention is better than a cure. If you don't lose your audience to begin with, then you won't have to figure out how you're going to bring them back.

- The best way to engage your audience is to prime them. Start by telling them what they're going to take away, what you expect them to learn, and what they are going to get out of the session. Remember WIIFT. Let them know up front, and then they're primed and ready so that when those key points come, it'll jog their memory and bring them back in and engage them anyway.

- Try to use these techniques and switch up how the presentation is going, whether that's an adjustment in visuals, a change using the four P's, physical movement on the stage, going from Point A to Point B, or doing something unexpected. Using those techniques every five to ten minutes can help prevent or alleviate brain drift.

- One of the easiest techniques you can use is to emphasize keywords. You can do that using gestures. You can do that using the four P's; however, you want to break up and emphasize key points. You can also add humor and emotion. Laughter is one of the best ways to hit the reset switch. If you can engage or introduce humor every five to ten minutes, it's naturally going to keep the engagement high.

- If you are at a point where the audience engagement is low, make fun of the situation. If you have a natural humor, that will help re-engage the audience. Anytime you're in doubt, interact with your audience in some form. For example, "Really quickly, I'm going to give you one, two, three, four, five, six, seven, eight, nine, ten. I'm giving you ten strategies, ten bullet points to re-engage your audience." If you're starting to lose them, those interactions can be to poll your audience either with a show of hands or with numbers.

- Verbally poll your audience, preferably with a question you already know the answer to because that will be a good transition for you to get into a new segment. Break for Q and A, and get them to write something down.

- Get your audience to verbalize something, or even involve them by asking, "If you're with me so far, raise your hand. Do it with me. Raise your hand and say, AYE."

- Change the energy. You'll re-engage your audience.

- If you're tech-savvy enough, have them take a poll on a smartphone. Almost everybody has a one nowadays. If you can, get them to take a poll, look up a stat, have them go to your website, or have them answer in a hashtag you have created. This raises your social media and speaker engagement and provides valuable information you can use in your presentation.

- The more you do these things, the easier it gets. The more you involve them, the more engaged they're going to be with you. Know the four P's inside and out: Power Pitch, Pause, Pace. Use them effectively and bring their focus back.

- The key is this: if you are losing your audience and you know it, feel it, and can sense it—do anything that changes the tone of the room and that will help you regain your audience's attention. All you have to do is change the tone of the room.

These are some of the strategies that have been most effective for me in my speaking career, and they have worked for my coaching clients as well. This is simply a buffet of ideas, so choose what works for you and discard the rest.

Engaging with your audience—and keeping them engaged—is critical to delivering your intended value to your audience. If you sense they are drifting, you now have tools you can use to bring everyone's attention back to you and your message.

Mind Ninja...
Secrets the Pros Don't
Want You to Know

In the last chapter, I discussed ways for you to get your audience interested and keep their focus on your message, as well as how to bring them back to you if they begin to drift away. Many of these methods focused on getting a response from the audience or having them participate in your presentation.

I will be discussing more ways to accomplish this goal in the current chapter, but the difference is that these strategies rely upon you and what you are doing within your talk, and not so much on what your audience will (or will not) do with you.

Here I will discuss seven more topics you can do to keep things a lot more interesting for your audience. These all play deep into our collective psyche and are wickedly effective if deployed and used correctly.

Silence

One of the greatest fears people have about speaking on stage is that they will forget what they are saying. The silence may feel eternal—seconds may feel like minutes or even hours. As a result, some speakers feel the need to keep talking and talking and talking—even to the point where they become a runaway train because they want to get everything out in the open before they forget anything.

There are several issues with this method. Fear of silence can cause a speaker to talk too fast, and therefore risk their message being lost completely. In addition, it can show a clear lack of confidence. As the authority on your subject, it can be uncomfortable for an audience to see you, as a speaker, struggle.

Finally, speakers fear silence because they are concerned about being judged negatively by others.

Rather than viewing silence as negative, choose to focus on the benefits instead. Picture your presentation as a conversation. When you are talking with a friend, there is a natural 'taking turns' protocol. When one person finishes a statement, that person waits for a response or reaction for the other person. It's like playing catch.

View speaking as a game, if it helps. When you are presenting, and you have said something impactful, wait a few seconds before continuing. Mel Robbins does this very well when discussing her 5 Second Rule on stage. I saw a speech where she was getting ready to introduce what the concept of the 5 Second Rule means. She said, "You're going to use the Five Second Rule, and what that means is this..." Her pause was ten seconds long— that is not an exaggeration. The audience was waiting to hear what she was about to say next. No-one assumed that she had forgotten her place because she hadn't. She used silence to make sure that everyone was fully engaged because she was about to give the main course—the meat of her speech.

Imitate Mel Robbins. Let the audience absorb what you say. In effect, let them catch up to you. That isn't possible when you are racing a thousand miles per hour. Silence is your friend.

Pause

Pausing is a form of silence, and you will want to do this periodically. The benefit is that you are encouraging your audience to participate. If you have asked a question during your presentation and you are looking for feedback, wait for someone to respond. Do not let the audience off the hook by answering the question for them. Let the quietness linger—someone will eventually feel the need to break the silence and speak up. If nothing else, pick a friendly face and ask that person how they might answer your question.

Using Your Voice to Project Confidence

Not only is what we say very important in our talk, but the way we say it has even more impact. If you want to project confidence, and therefore credibility, then you must realize that professionals use their voice as a tool to strategically emphasize their ideas. How can we emulate this strategy?

Any time we speak, there are usually three different tonalities that we can use: inflection up at the end of a sentence or question, flat inflection, or downward inflection. Each of these tones communicate differently, and being aware of this is critical to having a lasting impact on your audience.

When we speak with an upward inflection at the end of a sentence or question, it communicates a lack of confidence. In fact, it can make us seem like we are needy, needing validation, or wanting approval. When we use upward inflection at the end of a sentence, it sounds like we are asking a question when we really aren't, and it is an example of a speaker giving up power. This often happens when we are nervous. Our bodies are tense, and our vocal cords are not relaxed.

A perfect example of this comes from the movie American Pie. There is a girl who speaks the famous line "This one time...at band camp..." She used upward inflections constantly, even when speaking a statement and not a question. In fact, when a speaker is in the habit of using upward inflections, it becomes a hypnotic rhythm that's hard to break. You will likely lose your audience when you lull them into a pattern like this. Remember, the key to keeping an audience engaged is to not be predictable.

Another tonality we can use is a flat inflection. When we already have a rapport with someone, our tonality will not fluctuate as much because we are calm and comfortable—very much like talking to a close friend. However, in most cases, you will not already have a long-term rapport with your audience. A flat tonality can also be interpreted as monotone and boring, which is definitely not your desired outcome.

Finally, the last tonality is downward inflection. This indicates someone who has authority and is very confident. As a speaker, you want to project yourself as someone who knows the topic, has confidence, and owns the stage. In order to fully accomplish this, you will want to use downward inflections, or even flat inflections, as often as possible.

To practice this on your own, say, "How was your day?" in each of the three tonalities out loud and notice the difference in how you sound. You can record and listen to your own voice to notice how you sound. It may seem awkward at first, but the more you do it, the more natural it will sound.

The more confident you sound, the more influential you will be perceived to be. Clearly, this will help you communicate your message more effectively, and it will be received readily by your audience.

As an exercise, listen to well-known speakers—or speakers you want to emulate— and notice how they use tonalities in their presentations, make notes on how they do all the things discussed here, and then notice your confidence level in these speakers as you listen.

More About Transition Phrases

If you find that your audience is fading away, another thing you can do is use transition phrases in your talk. The purpose of a transition phrase is to signal a change of course or a movement to another topic within your speech. This will give your audience a chance to get back on board the train, so to speak.

Some excellent examples of this include:

"Let's move on to..."

"Now I'd like to discuss..."

"What I'd like you to do now..."

"I strongly recommend that…"

"What I want you to take away from…"

"The thought I'd like to leave you with…"

All these transition phrases serve the purpose of moving from one main idea in your presentation to another, and it signals movement. When an audience feels like you are moving toward a conclusion—even if you aren't there yet—they feel like your talk is progressing. It signals a change of pace, which is important because if a presentation is perceived as monotonous, the audience drifts away quickly. Perhaps the worst crime a speaker can commit is to be B-O-R-I-N-G. There is no recovery from that. The best way to make your transitional phrase obvious is to pause right before you deliver it. The pause serves as an alert, and the delivery of the transition is the signal to move to a new section of the speech.

Recap What You Just Told Them

One of the best things you can do in a presentation from a structural standpoint is to briefly review the main takeaways you want your audience to have at the end of each main point. If your talk has three main points, then at the end of each one simply re-cap the subject pertaining to that main point before moving on to the next idea.

For example, in my seminars, I frequently say something like, "By using these guidelines for memorizing substance instead of a script you will feel more confident when speaking, and you'll be able to make a more impactful connection with your audience because you won't be tied to reading slides."

This also serves as an obvious signal that you plan to move on to the next idea. When your audience knows there is an organized progression, it keeps members engaged even more.

Give People "Brain Food"

A lot of people overlook this, but the food and beverages that we feed ourselves can have a profound impact on concentration and alertness. One way to really stand out as a speaker is to focus not only on feeding your audience mind knowledge, but brain food as well.

If you have the budget, bring food items that will help people focus. Great examples of this would include almonds, walnuts, cashews, small cups of bananas and blueberries, dark chocolate, yogurt (without the sugar), green tea, and most importantly, water.

These foods and drinks will help your audience concentrate, which means they will be more engaged with you and retain more of your message.

Have an Excellent Close

I discussed this in an earlier chapter, but finishing well is very important because typically an audience will remember the first and last things you say. Even if your talk has not gone well, having an excellent close can salvage the situation. It can turn your talk around if it is impactful. If you can, you can use a call to action (CTA), which means you can invite them to visit a website for more information, download an app, text a number for a free gift, or even buy something in the back of the room (if permitted).

> A CTA is made by a speaker when the desired outcome is to buy something, do something, download something, or obtain any other intended result from the audience.

In order for the CTA to work well, you have to build a compelling case. Getting an audience to like you, know you, and trust you is a huge part of spurring them to act. You will never get someone to take action on anything you say if you haven't done that first. But assuming you have done that, your CTA can get your audience involved with you beyond the presentation and move them into your tribe of loyal followers or even loyal customers.

Clearly, if you are able to keep your audience engaged throughout the presentation, your chances of impact dramatically improve. But if you find that they have short attention spans, or if they get distracted by their own thoughts, these strategies can be very helpful in re-engaging their interest in what you are saying.

These ideas take some practice to implement. Anything worth doing well might be done badly the first few times you try it, but the payoff is well worth the effort. Study the top speakers, whether in person or on video. Pay attention to how they use each of these elements, and then try to emulate them as much as possible while maintaining your own authenticity. You don't want to be a copycat of someone else, but instead, you want to be the best possible version of you.

Your energy, your enthusiasm, and your personality can go a long way toward keeping an audience's attention. If it helps, be willing to let someone critique your performance. Have someone watch you practice, or even video record your talk and be willing to assess your own performance honestly. It's the best way for you to get better as a speaker, whether you are brand new at this or if you have years of speaking experience. All of us can get better, and the more willing we are to be vulnerable about that, the better off we are as speakers.

That's what speaking naked is all about.

Key Takeaways:

- Review the seven things that you can do to keep things interesting for your audience. These are all points that you can control and do not depend on the audience.

- Your voice is a powerful instrument which can project your authority and confidence. Study and practice using the three types of inflections, record yourself, and notice the differences. Use downward and flat inflections as often as possible.

- Use transition phrases to signal the end of one section and the beginning of the next. It is a great way to re-engage your audience and signal to them that your talk is moving forward.

- Having an excellent close is important. People most often remember the first and last thing we say. A strong finish will make your talk memorable.

Master Your Body,
Master Your Nerves

When I was in middle school at age fourteen, I had a chance to speak at a Remembrance Day ceremony, which is similar to what Veteran's Day would be in the United States. I had been speaking in public for eight years at that point because I had gotten started as a speaker when I was young. By this point, I had won multiple speaking competitions so anyone who asked me to speak knew they could rely on me to do a great job.

I was asked to read a famous Canadian poem called Flanders Fields by John McCrae. It was a huge honor because this poem gets read at every Remembrance Day ceremony. I had the opportunity to read this poem on three prior occasions, so I was comfortable with reading it again.

But this ceremony was different.

I remember seeing this grizzled, weathered veteran being brought to the front row in his wheelchair. He looked as if he had probably seen everything the world had to offer, good and bad. He was wearing all his medals and decorations, and he had a cane which he used to rest his chin on when he leaned forward in his wheelchair. He looked mean and bitter—there would be no smile on this man's face today.

In my head, he looked at me as if to say, "what are you going to do today to impress me, kid? You have no idea what I have seen in my lifetime." The enormity of what I was speaking about—what these veterans from the Greatest Generation went through—really struck me. Who was I to be reciting a poem to this man who had lived through war?

In that moment, I felt a pressure that I had never felt before or since. It was the first time I ever felt like I was being judged regarding my speaking.

I also have realized since then that an audience is not there to judge, and they aren't looking for a speaker to fail. Our minds will always project the worst-case scenarios upon us in an effort to protect us from going outside of our comfort zones.

This man wasn't mad at me, and he very likely was not thinking the things that I was projecting in my head, but that was the expression on his face, and I let it impact my speech.

The entire poem was gone. I couldn't recall it, and I didn't have a copy of it in front of me. I had recited this poem so many times that it didn't occur to me to have a backup plan.

Catch the lesson: Have a backup plan.

Even the most experienced speakers get nervous or have their moments of agony on stage. My story is an example.

Another example where a speaker let the moment overtake him was Transformers Director, Michael Bay. He was speaking on behalf of Samsung's new Ultra High-Definition Television at the Consumers Electronics Show in 2014. The teleprompter failed, and Bay told the audience he would "wing it" since the teleprompter wasn't working. Samsung's executive vice president was on stage with Bay and tried to assist him by asking for his opinion on their new television. Michael Bay simply froze, excused himself, and walked off stage.

The great lesson is that the moment can overtake any of us, so how should we cope when we get nervous?

When you are getting ready to speak, one of the best things you can do is be so prepared that you're ready for anything. This means that part of your preparation is to learn how to master your nervous energy. The reason I say nervous energy is that we all get anxious before we speak. Even the best speakers in the world experience some level of anxiety before hitting the stage.

> Getting nervous happens to the best of us.
> Have a strategy for handling anxiety.

Control That Nervous Energy

So, how do we control that nervous energy? There are a lot of techniques that you can use. One of the ways that I have learned to control this kind of energy is to look forward to the feeling. Believe it or not, I have trained myself to anticipate the high and the rush that comes from a well-delivered presentation. It's not something that I fear anymore. I look forward to those jitters, that excitement, that nervous energy that happens behind the stage. One of the best examples of somebody who can harness nervous energy is Tony Robbins. If you get a chance, watch *I'm Not Your Guru* and see what he does in his backstage warm-up. He has his little mini trampoline, and he stands there and jumps. He also does some amazing breath work.

That is the very first thing you need to do. Instead of being fearful of being on stage, train yourself to look forward to the opportunity. Here's the truth: the more you look forward to being nervous, the more you embrace it, and the more you're going to look for your speaking opportunities. It's a mindset that begets a more positive mindset. So, my first pro-tip is that you should look forward to speaking on stage.

Now, there are a couple of ways that you can do that. I'm going to share tips which I use that may work for you. Use the ones that speak to you, and throw away the rest.

Strategies

Affirmations

One of the things that I have done for a very long time is utilizing "I am" statements, which are back by science. There is a psychology behind constantly training your mind to think something. I write daily that I am a confident, powerful, authentic, engaging, highly paid international speaker. In particular, I stay focused on the "powerful, engaging, authentic speaker" section of that phrase.

What are some of the attributes that you aspire to be? Whether you already have them or not, those are the things that you'd want to put down in your I am's. So, if you want to be more confident, say "I am a confident speaker." We want to change the negative mindsets and reinforce the positive, and this is a powerful tool to begin to do this.

One of the other techniques that I use in order to get in the right mindset is to have a pre-talk routine. For the 15 to 20 minutes before your talk, do the same things consistently. For me, that is finding a quiet area in the auditorium and doing some breath work with visualization.

Piss on the Venue

I know speakers who metaphorically piss on the venue an hour or two before anybody is allowed into the auditorium or room where they're speaking. What that means is they will push every wall, touch every seat, and get a feel for the venue. They will make it their own, and they will even walk the stage. I love to walk the stage, and I recommend that you do that as well. If you get a moment to be on the stage prior to the audience there, it allows you to do a lot of visualization work, and with that visualization, you can get into a mindset where you can project yourself into the future. You can see the audience because it's easier since the seats are right there. If you can't get to the venue, see if you can get a picture of the space you will speak in. Take the time to focus and do some meditation on giving your talk. I'll discuss this a bit later.

Engaging with Your Audience

One of the other things I would strongly recommend—and this goes to being a good presenter and not simply harnessing nervous energy—is to not memorize a speech (I discussed earlier). If you do that, then you may get into the mindset of wondering what to do if you forget the script halfway through. I always break up my speeches into the five to ten bullet points that I want to cover.

When you have bullet points for your talk, you can put them up on stage, at the podium if there is one, or you can put them anywhere to guide you and center you. But if you are focused on memorizing an entire speech, you're simply inviting more nervousness. I used to act on stage and in film, and I wouldn't memorize the entire play. I would memorize my lines and then the lines that cued them. So, try to get away from recalling an entire speech. Instead, commit the concepts to memory. You will be more authentic.

You'll be able to engage with the audience because you won't be worried about which word or phrase comes next. You'll be able to share your story and your content in your own way. Of course, it will change each time, but that's great because if you have people who come to see you speak over and over and over again, then you're not giving the same speech repeatedly. You may be giving the same presentation, but it's never going to be the same talk—if that makes sense. That gives your audience a little bit of extra value, and then you have that feedback from them. Get away from the memorization, and that unto itself should help calm your nerves.

Play with your audience and be one with them. It's your one job to provide them with value, and the best way to provide them with value is to engage with them. By calming your nerves and not memorizing your speech, you will be able to then interact with and provide them with better value. That's a better experience for both parties involved, so stay focused on the audience. Instead of focusing on how you feel, focus on how the audience feels. Focus on what you can do to pick up on their cues, and if you learn to read your audience, then the nervousness factor disappears because you can only concentrate on one thing.

If you concentrate on your audience by making sure that you're reading your cues, looking around, and making sure that you are providing content and value, then you don't have to worry about what you're doing. It's about providing a great experience, focusing on your audience and having a conversation with them. Even if you pick one person in the audience, you were able to look at him or her, focus and really be able to calm yourself that way.

Some people suggest that you picture your audience naked. I have never really understood that advice or what purpose it serves. Another thing people suggest is to look above your audience's heads. Why would you do this? Instead, look people in the eye.

Really connect with them, and you will be able to get a feel for how you are doing.

> Pro-tip: If an audience has come to see you, they don't want to see you fail. That's usually every speaker's biggest fear. The audience is on your side!

Audiences don't know you have a fear of failing, and that's the other great thing about going with bullet points rather than memorizing your speech. They don't know what you're going to say. Even if you've given your talk multiple times, they *still* don't know what you're going to say. Nobody I know has ever gone to a talk and said, "I hope this speaker sucks, wouldn't it be great if they bomb." You've never done that. I've never done that. That's not the way that humanity works. We go to hear speakers waiting to be wowed. That's your moment. That's your opportunity, so get the negativity of projected expectation of failure out of your mind. That audience is there to see you succeed because you are the expert. They're here to see you. They are already there in support of you, and they want to see you succeed.

Go in focused on success. You are in an auditorium with 4, 400, or even 40,000 people, and they're there to see you succeed. So, when you're doing your mental prep, picture the love and the energy of your entire audience there to see you rock your speech. You have their support before you ever get on stage, and when you get onstage, they continue with that support. All you have to do is be there and give them the content that you promised to maintain their support. Give them the experience they came for and they will continue to love you. Focus on that and embrace the nervous energy. Start to love it and know that your audience is there for you, and you are there for them. Love the audience, and all of a sudden it becomes a positive experience. You being on stage is positive instead of negative. You don't need to be afraid.

Breathing Exercises

Another great thing you can do to master your body is to breathe. If you have done any form of meditation, you might be familiar with Prana Breath; it's one of the techniques that I have learned to use. It's a subset of a tantric work. If you want to know the science behind Tantra, breathing, or meditation, there are a lot of resources. Reach out to me, and I can send you that information. It's about breath and connection. As a speaker, we want to connect with our audience and, in a larger sense, with our world which is what got me into the breathing exercises. Remember when I was talking about how some speakers will touch things in the room, and they will touch the walls and the chairs? I don't do it physically, but instead, I do it metaphorically.

I like to breathe my energy into the room, so I will do my meditations prior to it on the stage if I can. If not, I will do it backstage, and I will breathe my energy into the room. That's how I get started. I want to extend my energy out into the area so that it is now my space, and I get to welcome people into my zone and give them an experience.

The way that I do it is through Prana Breath, and I use three different cycles. Typically, a breathing meditation will be seven to ten minutes, sometimes as long as fifteen. I like to do three cycles in seven-minute segments so that it takes up my twenty to twenty- one minutes of prep time prior to going on stage.

The order of my three breathing meditations is that I clear my mind, I calm my body, and then I finish with power breathing. With a clear mind, it's simple breaths in and out. With Prana Breathing, it doesn't matter if you're breathing in through the nose and out through the nose, or in through the nose, out through the mouth. The key is you're not going to breathe in through the mouth.

Now, with a clear mind, it's simple breaths in, and then out. But what you do is change the timing on the inhalation versus the exhalation. Take three seconds to breathe in and then take nine seconds to breathe out. Now, when you're breathing out, you want to do a full exhale. Work through the diaphragm and breathe in from there, then fill up your lungs. When you breathe out, start from the lungs and then finishing by collapsing your diaphragm. That's the cycle: in out, in out. I use a metronome to keep a consistent and steady pace that is set to sixty beats per minute, which is one beat per second. I listen to it—tick, tick, tick—and then I count in my head, one, two, three, one, two, three, four, five, six, seven, eight, nine.

It helps that I'm a drummer, but if you're doing that correctly, you're going to have a total of five breaths per minute. If you're breathing in for three seconds out for nine, that's a total of twelve seconds. Twelve seconds divided by sixty, five breaths per minute. That is what I do to clear my mind.

The next breathing pattern I use is 'calm', and it's a little bit of a different cycle. It's three seconds in, six seconds hold, three seconds out, six seconds hold, but here's the hitch. It's like a singer's breath. A lot of these techniques are used by professional singers and vocalists, and they have power in their voice. So, when they talk, they project from the diaphragm. That's why we want to breathe in through the diaphragm because if you get used to doing that—and if you're doing it for twenty minutes prior to going on stage—your body naturally wants to start breathing in from the diaphragm. Suddenly you're breathing in that manner. You're supporting your voice. When I do this, all of a sudden, I'm really loud and can fill an auditorium without actually ever having to breathe.

I can probably sustain thirty seconds of talk in one breath because

I supported the breath through the diaphragm, and I very rarely use a mic in large auditoriums. In a small auditorium that fits 500 seats or less, I'm all me all the time, and I've never really had a problem. That's why we're talking about breathing because it is so effective. It will support your breath very much like a singer, and you're able to speak and project for longer periods of time.

So, the calm breath works like this: you'll take three breaths. Breathe in for three seconds, then hold it for six seconds, and then exhale for three seconds. Continue this cycle for seven minutes.

Let's explore this a little further. After you do your initial breath intake for three seconds, you'll want to sustain that breath within your cavity for six full seconds. Then breathe out for three seconds, releasing all the way. About 90% of your air should come out in those three-second breaths out, and then again, sustain for six. You have to be calm doing that because otherwise, you're going to metabolize the oxygen within your system. That's why it's calming, because you need to control that breath so that when you are in those plateaus—both above and below, breath in and breath out—you're able to control your body and control your oxygen. Again, it's backed by science. You can look into it, but know this technique will work. It will force you to calm down. If you do that for seven minutes, you will have taken three and a half breaths per minute, so you're slowing your breathing down significantly. Now let's explore power breathing. I like to move into power because, again, I like to bring my energy out into the room. If you take that power and if you get into the mindset, then this is when you can really start focusing on your breath, focusing on your venue, focusing on your audience, what you want to do, and what you want to deliver to them.

The breath cycle for power is three seconds breathing in, six seconds sustaining, and then six seconds breathing out. After you breathe in, you're always sustaining with the full chest so that you're taking in more than you're letting out. Three seconds in, six seconds sustain, and then six seconds out and you repeat.

There is a free app is called Prana Breath which can help you breathe with this process. When you play it, you get some nice chimes that will help you count the timing of your breathing. Use it if it works for you, or discard it if it doesn't. I only suggest this because I have found that it works for me. If it works for you, great. If not, toss it over your shoulder and move on.

Proper breathing can really help you center yourself prior to your talk, and it will calm your nerves. It lets you operate from a place of having a clear and calm mind, and it allows you to claim your power so you can more effectively serve your audience.

When you give a presentation, you will need to pay attention to your voice and your physical presence. Let's discuss these now.

Voice

The interesting thing about live presentations is they aren't always perfect, and that's the other reason why we practice. The more you practice, and the more comfortable you are with your material, the more you can take those odd scenarios and off the cuff situations and be successful among them. So, when you're practicing, stay focused on your voice. Record yourself, see where the inflections are, see where the notes are, and see where tonality comes in and out. If something sounds off because you are working on a serious talk, it could be that you're nervous, so your voice pitch goes a little higher, and you don't sound like you normally would. Practicing will make you aware of this so that you can avoid those pitfalls and become more comfortable. If nervousness is an issue, awareness is the first step, and practicing will help. On a side note, if anybody has ever seen me present live, I very seldom speak with a microphone. I've been in theater since I was six years old, so I've learned how to operatically support with my diaphragm and project my voice. When I do this, I have absolutely no problem filling a 500-seat auditorium with my voice and have people hear me clearly.

But not everybody can do that. That said, if you're working with a mic, practice with it, if possible. Keep in mind that just because you have a mic doesn't mean that you don't need to speak loud. Speak comfortably. Don't shout into the mic, but work with your sound tech. Ask them about the equipment and really learn. A good friend of mine, John E. Fraser at Zen AV Services, is a tech guru and an amazing resource when it comes to sound, visuals, and room set up. Follow his blog for some incredible pro tips on mic work and A/V gear.

As I have gained experience, I have learned the technical side of speaking, beyond being able to skillfully present using the five P's. The technical component is important, but it is often overlooked. That being said, it really would be beneficial when you're practicing with a mic to find that opportunity to work with the sound engineer who is going to be running the soundboard so that they can explain what you need to know and help you get comfortable.

As an example, if I have a lavalier mic, I can't have it really close to my mouth. I know to tell the sound guy, "You want it back on my jaw bone and trust me because

I've done this," and we'll run a mic test. They usually know the best place for my mic to be situated. You don't want to have it too high or too low from your mouth, or too close or too far away. Ask the sound tech before you speak, and practice so that you are prepared to have the best sound quality available for your talk. The majority of people hold a mic too far away, so preparation and practice are really important.

Mic placement is also imperative because if you talk too softly, or if your mic is too far away from you, people might miss your magnificent message and all your preparation will have been wasted. Practicing and doing a technical rehearsal will make a huge difference and save you from unforeseen issues that can be avoided. Don't let your first time on a new stage be the actual delivery of your presentation. Keep all these things in mind. Executing them comes with practice. Do a short run through with your tech crew. At least try to scope out what the equipment is, or better yet, do what I do and travel with your equipment yourself, so there are no issues.

Of course, none of this matters if you aren't speaking and enunciating your words clearly, so be mindful of that as well. Make sure the audience can hear and understand everything you are saying. You might find that recording yourself practicing your talk will help. I know a lot of people don't like hearing their own voice, but being willing to get uncomfortable is critical to achieving your greatest outcomes, so record and listen to yourself first. Recording yourself can also help you be aware of filler words, and not only "um" or "you know" but rather the idiosyncrasies that may have crept in. For me, it was "you guys" for a long time, or I would finish my sentences with "right?" Practicing will only help you eliminate those phrases from your talk.

> Speak at a comfortable pace, not too fast or too slow.

Another thing to be aware of is the pace of the presentation. Many speakers talk too fast, and that comes from nervous energy. When in doubt, slow down. Remember to breathe and relax. Having a solid pre-talk routine will help tremendously—and we will address that in detail later on.

Closely related to how fast you talk is the use of pauses at strategic points during your presentation. I mentioned this earlier. One very important reason to pause occasionally is to let the audience "catch up" to what you are saying, especially if you are giving a lot of great content. They are likely hearing your information for the first time while you are used to delivering this message over and over again, so they will need time to process what you are saying. Another important reason to pause is for dramatic impact. If you have shared something serious, you should consider pausing for an extra second or two and let your message sink in.

Physical Presence

Physical presence and body language are important to how you are perceived as a speaker, and therefore important to your success on stage. How you stand and how you move will affect the quality of your voice, and a lot of people aren't aware of that. So anytime you have an opportunity to practice your entrance on and off the stage, do it. Any chance that you have to be in a room and see if you can fill that with your voice, do it. If you get the chance to video and record yourself giving a presentation so that you can see what your quirks and ticks are, take that opportunity as well.

I coach a lot of professional speakers, and a lot of my clients— even well-known speakers—still occasionally get that weird nervous pace during their talks. It looks like they're either trying to practice for the Tour de France, and they're pedaling in one place, or they don't lift their feet and then look like a weird two- step shuffle like they need to pee. A lot of us do things like this subconsciously. Until we can actually watch the video playback and look ourselves, a lot of those physicalities go unnoticed. The more you record yourself in a speaking situation, the more you are aware of the quirks of your own vocal and physical stylings.

Seeing the room before you speak will also give you an idea of whether or not there is a podium or lectern, and whether or not it will remain on stage or can be removed.

I personally like to move around on stage, but I do it with purpose. Moving around at random doesn't serve your message. Instead, if you plan to move around, do so as you begin your next point or next story. This represents a very clear pattern interrupt and can signal the audience to pay attention again if they have faded.

One great suggestion to rid yourself of nerves is to zone in on a few trustworthy faces and give eye contact throughout the talk. I had mentioned this in a previous chapter. Looking people in the eye gains trust between you and your audience. You want your audience to feel connected to you, so focusing on a point on the wall won't help.

In addition, the use of gestures can add to your presentation as long as they serve a constructive purpose. Use gesture to express your ideas or to emphasize something you are saying. Clapping or raising your hands are good examples of this. Be aware of random gestures, and watching a recording of yourself can help you with this. You might be doing things you didn't even notice. Also, if you watch experienced speakers, notice how they gesture. I promise, it's always for a reason which advances their message.

Pre-Talk Routine

I've gotten to be a powerful, confident, and engaging speaker as a result of my pre-talk routine.

I suggest you get a pre-talk routine for yourself that sets you up to give the best of yourself to your audience. I know other speakers who, as part of their breathing exercises, take water at certain times. They'll have their Nalgene bottle, and they know that they're going to drink four fluid ounces twenty minutes prior, and then another two sips before they go on. They do that so that they're not overly hydrated so that they would need to pee on stage, but that they have a nice, good sustained vocal cord. I know some speakers that will do a full-on meditation where they're not only doing Prana Breaths, but also meditating on the talk through some powerful visualization. Personally, I do my visualizations a couple of days before the talk to get into the mindset, and then on the day of the talk, I'm focused on me and the energy in the room. But again, you and only you can come up with your routine. Here's the thing: just like a professional athlete—or any professional for that matter—if you're going to develop that routine, keep it consistent and keep it the same. You may experiment occasionally, with adding or subtracting things, but don't get radical about it. Once you get into it, you want to make sure that you have that routine because the whole point is building something that promotes comfort and confidence. You want to master your body and your nerves. If we're going to know ourselves and really get into our mind, we want to make it a happy, comfortable place. Therefore, find yourself a routine that works for you, steal any ideas from me that you want, and discard the ones that you don't want to work with when you're on stage.

In the next chapter, I will give you a deeper dive into how I specifically construct my pre-talk routine

Now You're on Stage

We've discussed the pre-talk preparation, so now let's talk about going on stage. One of the things that I can't stress enough is that you have to believe in you during those first three seconds. If you don't believe in yourself, you lose the audience. This whole pre- routine we discussed is to get you in the mindset that you're going to crush it. If you don't believe it, simply know that I believe you are going to be amazing.

You need to get in that mindset. You need to know that this audience is there to love you, and that they're there to support you. They want to see you succeed. You are the expert. You are why they are there. You own that stage. So, you need to walk onto that stage like you own it, and if you're like me and you run your own talks, guess what? You rented the space. You've paid for it, so you own that stage for a little bit. This always helps me. If I rented this venue for X number of dollars, then I own the stage. For however many days or hours, it's mine. Walk in with confidence because that stage is yours. You need to walk to your mark, and you need to own it. You need to stand like you belong there—because you do. One of the greatest rewards you can give yourself is when you walk out to the stage and take your mark, take a second and soak it all in. I do this. It may feel uncomfortable at first, and it may be uncomfortable for the audience, but if you go out with confidence, give the audience a grin and make some eye contact with people, you will feel more energized, relaxed and engaged, I promise. The key to this is to remember you want to be on that stage, and your audience wants you there too.

It's your moment, your stage. They're there for you, and that's where you start that connection with them. Find some people in the audience who are giving you that love back, and you can anchor yourself to them. Tell yourself, "OK, let's do this thing." Then launch into your talk. You really must master that walk onto the stage, master that strut. Want to work on it with me? I will Facebook, Facetime, Skype, Zoom, what ever with you, and as weird as it sounds, I'll watch you walk, and I'll tell you if I think you're walking with confidence. This is something I do for my coaching clients, and I would be happy to discuss coaching with you if you want to level up your speaking game.

If you feel like you're walking way too slow, you're probably walking just about right. When you take your mark, you center yourself and ground yourself in that spot. Don't stand on one leg or lean on a wall. Be grounded, be centered. Plant yourself in one place, and then you are ready to begin.

> Stay in one place for the first two minutes of your talk. This focuses the audience on you.

When you're doing your talk, I challenge you to not move for the first two minutes. You can use your hands, but your feet stay grounded and planted. The next time you talk, see if your nerves magically disappear because you have to think about standing still. If you have nervous energy, you're going to pace back and forth without purpose. How many times have you seen somebody do that? It's distracting, isn't it? Not only that, but it is exhausting both for your audience having to track you and physically for you as well. You are expending energy unnecessarily when you pace, so staying grounded and centered will help you conserve energy that you can then give to your audience.

If you can mentally be aware that this is what you're doing, then choose to stay grounded for the first two minutes of your talk, whether it's ten minutes, fifteen minutes, two hours, or even the whole day so your audience is with you right from the start— guaranteed. This one strategy, being grounded at the beginning and not moving, means they have to focus on you. They're not going to focus on anything else because you have them. You've got them grounded because you're grounded. So, if you can do that for two minutes, you're going to have yourself a fantastic talk because you won't even know that you're nervous anymore due to this strategy. You will have calmed yourself down, and that's the whole point. Master your body, master your nerves. It's a matter of finding breath control, finding those ticks within yourself, and mastering your body.

You can master your body. It doesn't have the choice to be nervous because you tell your body what it's going to do. If you tell yourself, "I love speaking. I love the high. I get off on the love of the audience. I love going out and doing this"—this is energy that you are creating. This is energy that allows you to grab your audience. You control your body. You control what is 'nerves' and what is energy. You tell that energy what it's going to do and give it to your audience. Give them the love, and they're going to love you back. So, stand up straight. Take some deep breaths. Look people in the eye. Smile. You're there to have some fun, even if you're giving a serious talk.

My friend Jared Morrison's Ten Minute Time Machine presentation is one of the most serious talks you'll ever hear in your life. The topics that he talks about—suicide, depression, the collapse of family relationships—hits the heart in a heavy way. Do you know what Jared does? He smiles and draws his audience in because he's got an unmistakable charisma about him. As a result, Jared gives them permission to feel whatever they want to feel— and then he makes it OK. He makes it safe because he turns around and smiles again. He makes them laugh. So, don't be afraid to smile.

> Smile—the energy you give is the energy you receive.

Regardless of your topic, you should smile at the beginning and the end because before you open your mouth and after you say goodbye, your audience should be clapping for you. If they're doing that, you have permission to smile—get serious in the middle, but don't forget to smile.

I want to say one more thing about being grounded. When you take your walk on stage, don't ground yourself behind a podium. It's a barrier between you and your audience.

How many speakers do you see who stand behind a podium? They do this even if they're not reading off their notes or have their speech memorized. This does nothing for the audience. They can't see half of you. The only thing this does is mask the fact that you might have peed in your pants. So, don't stand behind the podium. In fact, if you can, ask them to get rid of it or have it off to the side. If the podium has to remain on stage and has to be centered, take a casual stance beside it and then move away. The podium is a physical barrier between you and your audience and takes you away from your purpose, which is to connect with your audience and give them value.

Finally, when you are on stage, you want to own your space. Our nonverbal communication determines how we are judged and perceived. When we use open or expansive gestures, it expresses power and confidence. Think about an athlete that wins a race. When he crosses the finish line, he raises his arms in a V sign for victory. On the other hand, when someone loses, their body language can contract and close in.

When we are on stage speaking, we can own our power by being very open with our gestures. Our words also need to match our 'nonverbals' or the message no longer makes sense. An audience will evaluate us based on nonverbal communication even more than on the words we say. Being passionate, authentic, comfortable, and enthusiastic helps a lot. Therefore, it is important to possess all these qualities not only verbally, but nonverbally as well. This allows us to be the authority on stage.

When you put all these things together, it will make a huge difference in your presentation and how it is received. In turn, that determines the impact we will have with our audience.

That's a winning combination.

Key Takeaways: ——————————————————

- Pressure enhances performance, so learn to embrace the pressure. Pressure is the thing that will make you succeed. Learn to love it. Learn to love the excitement, learn to love the nerves and learn to look forward to it, and then you get to be sick in the head like me and want to do this for a living.

- Focus on your audience. If you focus on them, you're not focused on you. You are engaging them, and now they are having a better time. That means you are serving them the way that you promised to, so focus on your audience.

- If you want to do breathing exercises before your talk, consider using Prana Breath. If not, don't. But have a pre-talk routine. Do something that is only for you, that gets you in the right mindset to be able to serve your audience to the fullest capacity.

- Stand straight. Walk on stage like you own that space. You know that your audience is there to support you and they love you. They're not judging you. They want you to succeed. Be conscious of your gestures and get away from the podium.

If you can master your body and master your nerves, speaking will be an all-around amazing experience not only for you but for your audience as well. In the next chapter, I will talk about developing your pre-talk routine in much more detail. Let's continue.

How to Develop A
Pre-Talk Routine

have talked about mastering your body and mastering your nerves. One of the many aspects of this is having a pre-talk routine, which I want to explore in more depth in this chapter.

Why is this so important? It provides a foundation to be centered and grounded prior to speaking. You may not always be able to control what goes on once you hit the stage, but you can always control what happens before the moment of truth arrives. Therefore, I'm going to share how to develop a pre-talk routine and how to get into the mind-set to be able to go out and rock the stage.

Components of A Great Pre-Talk Routine

Rehearse

First things first. One of the first things you can do as part of a pre- talk routine is the 'pre' pre-talk routine. This means rehearse, rehearse, rehearse, rehearse. I can't stress enough the importance of rehearsal from a technical stand-point so that you know what you're doing when you get onto the stage. As discussed earlier in the book, doing a tech rehearsal prior to doing your talk ensures that every-thing goes according to plan and you don't have to catch up 'on the fly'.

Get into the habit of rehearsal, because things then become instinctual, they're ingrained in you, and you can go on defaults.

Mark Your Territory

Along with rehearsing, one of the things that you can do as far as a pre-talk is to get into the mindset of pissing on the stage. I mentioned this earlier.

Now, don't take that literally. But think about this for a second. Animals mark their territory, right? They spray on things. Well, this is what I want you to do. An effec-tive pre-talk routine is to go and touch everything in the room or the theater or the auditorium. Wherever you're presenting, go in and physically touch the walls. Touch the stage, touch the chair, get your DNA all over everything.

Visualize yourself in your talk and what you're doing on the stage. Visualize the audience when it's full. It's a nice stress relief, and it's very tactile for anybody who needs that to calm down. If you're fidgety, walk around and touch things, it's very helpful.

Get Active

Another part of your pre-talk routine can be to get active. In those thirty minutes, or even sixty minutes before your talk, do something that gets your blood pumping and gets the endorphins up. For example, you can do jumping jacks. Think of Tony Robbins behind the stage on his mini trampoline. He gets his heart pumping by jumping up and down immediately prior to going on stage. He gets himself amped up, and then boom, Tony takes the stage. This is an awesome routine to see live in person, by the way, if you ever are lucky enough to be backstage to see Tony in his pre-talk routine.

Another great way to get active is to mark your territory fast, meaning touching everything in the auditorium, the theater, or the room that you're in and get your heart rate up while doing so. If you're doing any merchandising on your own, then put out any flyers, promo material, or any worksheets yourself beforehand. It lets you experience the whole venue before you speak.

If you're speaking to large groups, and you have a crew helping you, get out and get that stuff prepped along with your team. It shows great camaraderie. It gets them going, and you can make it a competition to see who can get the materials out the fastest. It's a great pre-talk routine method. As always, all the things that I'm suggesting are for you to take or leave. Use what works, and leave the rest.

Later in this chapter, I'm going to take you through what my pre- talk routine is, but these are all suggestions for you. It's up to you to develop your own routine that makes sense to you. Develop something that gets you into the mindset to deliver the most powerful talk that you can.

Meditate, Breathe, Visualize

I mentioned getting active. The next thing that you can do about 20 minutes before your talk is some meditation and real deep breathing; a couple of deep breaths, seconds before you go on stage, is also very helpful at calming your nerves.

If you're somebody who's nervous before you go on and speak, taking some deep breaths in is a very effective tool for a couple of reasons. First of all, it has a psychological effect on your nervous system. The reason it has a psychological effect on this system is because the hypothalamus is linked with the endocrine system. What happens is that your brain is talking to your nervous system, and it emits hormones, more specifically neurohormones, that trigger a relaxation response. Try it right now. Take three deep breaths. You'll already start to calm after the first one. Then take two more.

This triggers your brain, and it's a pattern interrupt as well, so taking a couple of deep breaths brings your nerves down. It also helps you center and calm yourself. Do this twenty minutes before your talk. If you take some breaths along with meditation, this allows you to really focus on and visualize your talk. Now, whether you do that in meditation, visualization is also a powerful tool as part of both a pre-talk routine and rehearsal routine. So, visualizing yourself onstage, visualizing your audience, visualizing the impact that you want to have, really taking time to center in on you, delivering the most powerful message and impact on your audience is powerful. This can be profound and can really set up a positive experience in your mind. If you combine that with your meditation, it can be very powerful even if you're only doing it as part of the visualization exercise.

I like to combine the two. So as part of my meditation, I will include a visualization of me delivering my talk. I know a lot of people who have some nerves or jitters when they're talking in front of a group. If you are one of them, I assure you that it's completely normal. What I want you to do is to remember that not only is the breathing and visualization a great way of changing your mindset, but rehearsing and practicing help as well.

I want you to start looking forward to the high and to look forward to the nerves. I was doing an interview with Manny Wolfe on a podcast recently, and we were talking about first kisses. When you kissed someone for the first time—and I mean your first kiss ever—were you scared or nervous? I was terrified and I remember it to this day. It's imprinted on my mind and it was wonderful. I loved my first kiss, but I was terrified. The first time I went in for it, my heart was pumping, and my hands were sweating. It's comparable to everything that we feel when we go onstage. You're frightened and nervous, but when you lean in and go for it, then it can be awesome. You'll want it to do it again and again.

That's the mindset that I want you to get in when it comes to speaking. Part of that visualization is looking forward to that high, to that excitement because, let's face it, you've had other first kisses with new people; now you know what's coming and you're looking forward to the experience. That's the mindset that I want you to get to where your thoughts are, "I get to speak in front of 3000 people today. I get to speak in front of 10,000 people today!" How many of you read that and thought, "I can't imagine talking in front of 10,000 people." I look forward to it. Why? Because it gives me a high. Just like kissing, I want more.

I love the surge. I love the energy. I love feeling a room. I love big crowds. They excite me in a way that I can't even begin to articulate, which is ironic because I'm a speaker. So flip your mindset and get into the routine to start to look forward to it. Create a mantra before you go on the stage.

For example, "I am looking forward to this crowd. I'm excited to present to this crowd. I'm excited to give my presentation. I'm excited to feel the energy of the audience instead of being scared or nervous." Let yourself feel those statements. Get excited. Think about this: whether you are excited or anxious, the physiological response within your body is exactly the same. So let's flip the language with it, and then you will start to look forward to that presentation.

Work the Room

> Pro-Tip: As part of your pre-talk routine, if you can work it in, you can chat with your audience right at the entrance.

You will find opportunities to build relationships in advance of your talk if you can take time to greet people as they arrive.

Introduce yourself and be the first one to say something. For example, I might say, "Hi, I'm Sean Tyler Foley. I'm the one who's presenting the talk today. What brought you here today?" Work your audience, and this will let you do a couple of things. It lets you gage who's in your audience so you can craft your message just a little bit better. You can start to tailor and hone your delivery. It also gives you a sense of who's there. It gives you a chance to get personal anecdotes as well. You can ask, "Tell me a little bit about yourself. What do you do? Why'd you come to the talk today? What excited you about it?" And then if you have a story that parallels where you can bring them in, that's instant engagement because now you're personalizing to your audience. So, if you can work a meet and greet into your pre-talk routine, work the room prior to going on stage.

How can you effectively work the room before your talk?

There's a great framework known as F.O.R.D. that is easy to use. As you can probably guess, that's an acronym you can use to make things easier to remember. Each letter in the acronym stands for a cluster of topics that nearly everyone should relate to. Let's look at this closer.

F=Family

Using stories and examples that involve family can be a great way to help people know, like and trust you. It can add a personal touch and get your audience to identify with you. If you can share success stories that involve family members, it's even better. The stage isn't the place to air your dirty laundry about them.

O=Occupation

Discussing work or school-related items is very normal, as studies show that 45% of our time is spent in there. It's very non- threatening and can be another great way to build rapport. If your occupation is speaking full-time, stories from the road may be appropriate. Even if your full-time work involves something else, you may be able to share stories if they relate to your topic.

If you are speaking at an event for an industry that is familiar to you (i.e., health care, real estate, financial), you can share stories that directly related to your audience's industry. If nothing else, it will give the appearance that you have done some research and that you have relevant things to share for that specific audience.

R=Recreation

Everyone has a hobby, interest, or passion that they spend time on outside of their occupation. If appropriate, you could share something related to one of your interests during the talk. Better yet, if you have a chance to mingle before your talk, ask a few people what they are passionate about and try to weave that into your talk somehow. It shows a genuine interest in connecting during your presentation.

D=Dream

Dreams can be very powerful because everyone has something they have always thought about achieving. When you share stories about how you or someone else achieved something significant, it can help audience members believe that they can also reach their goals, especially when you share what that achievement took to accomplish. In fact, when some of your stories are centered on someone else other than yourself, there is proof that anyone can do it. When you make your stories relatable, it resonates with your audience more.

Now, working the room like this doesn't work for everybody. Can you imagine if somebody like Phil Town, Brian Tracy, Darren Hardy, Tony Robbins, or even Oprah started walking through the room prior to their talk? Part of their presentation is the excitement and the buildup of the fact that they are about to take the stage. So, it may not work for you, but in my case, I find it incredibly effective because I can personalize my message and tailor it for that specific situation. For me, walking the room prior and getting a sense of who's there is very beneficial for me, and you may be able to work that into your pre-talk routine as well.

Stay Hydrated and Have A Vocal Routine

Our final point before we get to what my pre-talk routine is that you need to stay hydrated. Drink some water, but not a lot. Think about why that's not a good idea. If you pound back two liters of water just before you go onstage, then what's likely to happen in about fifteen minutes into your talk? You know I don't have to say it, right? You also want to hydrate so you don't get dry lips which makes it more awkward to talk. In fact, Google the benefits of drinking water, as there are many. But for a speaker, you'll need to hydrate your instrument because that's important.

It helps calm the nerves. It's also great for memory retention, so it'll help you with your recall. It will even help with balance. The benefits of staying hydrated should be very evident.

One of the other things that you can incorporate into your pre-talk is a vocal routine. Warming up is critical. Singers do this before taking the stage, and all the great speakers do as well. If you are somebody like me who takes great pride in their ability to project and fill a room without a mic, I am only able to do that because I do a proper vocal warm-up. And there are some excellent ones on YouTube. My favorite is a TED talk that Julian Treasure presented where he goes through a series of exercises that really engage all the components of the mouth.

I used to do those kinds of vocal warm-ups when I was in musical theater, so I've adopted a lot of my stagecraft practices to my speaking vocal warm-up. I do this to get my voice ready. I play with the tone of my voice, too. Your vocal warm-ups may depend on who the audience is. In my experience, if I am speaking to a youthful audience and I need to be a little bit more playful, my voice rises. I tend to take on a little bit more youthful tone. If it's an older crowd, or if I'm presenting in a very professional manner (i.e., one of my safety talks), then I take on a little bit more authoritative and lower pitched tone. I also slow down my cadence a little bit, and all of this is because I do my vocal warm- ups.

Let's summarize what we've discussed so far. Part of your pre-talk routine is getting in the mindset, knowing who the audience is, and how the information needs to be presented. Rehearse and practice ahead of time, get active, 'piss on the room' or mark your territory. Breathe or meditate (or both) twenty-five minutes before your talk, and then again immediately before you take the stage. Take a couple of breaths to get calm, centered, and focused. Don't forget to do power visualizations within that hour prior to your talk. Flip your mindset so that you're looking forward. Be excited about giving your talk, and chat up the audience beforehand. If you can get in there and work the room prior to delivering your talk, that's ideal. Finally, remember to hydrate and do vocal warm-ups. I gave some great examples of vocal warm-ups in an earlier chapter.

My Specific Pre-Talk Routine

My pre-talk routine goes a little something like this: I like to get to the venue the day before as part of the setup, so if I can, like I said, I will do my own seat drops, or pamphleting on seats, and set up if I'm able to. That only works if there are no other speakers that day except me. So, when I'm doing, for example, a two-and-a-half-day workshop or facilitation, I will get there the day before, and I help my crew merch the chairs, the tables, or the setup just so that I can get active and in the room. I like to mark my territory. I like to do it, not for the nervous energy, but for allowing me to check my sight lines so that I can see if somebody's sitting at various strategic spots throughout the room, how well can they see the stage and help me asses if there are issues I need to know about.

A walk-through also allows me a chance to do a tech set up. I'll put on my lavalier microphone, and I'll walk around to check the sound quality. It's important for me to know how my voice sounds to the audience, and now the power of wireless mics enables me to do just do that. It also allows me to do a tech check for any music cues that I have, as well as any lighting cues. So, if I do have lights or if I have a presentation that I'm working from, I get to test the tech, and I do that a day before. Then on the day of the presentation, I do a quick tech rehearsal again, to make sure that nothing got bumped in the night. If machines have been shut down, it's a chance to get them powered back up.

It's also very important to do a mic test and make sure that you have batteries. Here's a pro-tip on batteries. On meal breaks or at the end of the day, I always change battery packs. I had a fellow speaker mention to me that I should change the batteries right before I go on stage. Of course, you want to make sure the batteries you are using are good, but he suggested that at the beginning of the day and during meal breaks, change the batteries and always use the good ones. As a result, I make sure to do a mic check just before I go on. Once I have done this, I watch to see when audience members start coming into the room. And if I can, I like to work the room a little bit and thank them for coming.

I'll ask questions such as, "How did you hear about this event? What are you looking forward to? What else have you done? Who are you? What do you do?" I'll get those personal anecdotes so that I can start to craft and tailor some of the messages so that I can really speak to that audience. Then about thirty-five to forty minutes before my talk, I get backstage, and I get to a quiet place where I can make silly noises—just warming up, getting my body moving and active—and I will do that for probably ten or fifteen minutes. Then I get quiet and do my meditation. I go through three Prana Breath cycles.

I've talked about this before, and it's all about relaxing and calming the nerves. As I previously mentioned, the three Prana Breath cycles are calm, relaxed, and then power. The power one is where you're drawing in more breath than you're letting out. What I'm visualizing is me putting my energy out to the room because ultimately that's my job.

I need to serve the room so before I take the stage, I start to calm, I start to visualize, and while I'm doing my progress in that cycle, I do three distinct breathing patterns which are seven minutes long. So that's twenty-one minutes in that I'm visualizing what I'm doing, how I'm delivering my talk, and what I'm going to do. That gives me about four minutes prior to taking the stage, and one more opportunity to shake out my body and loosen up. Then when I'm about a minute to taking the stage, I take a couple of sips of water. I also make sure that either my crew or I have set up a couple of waters on stage and that I have my podium ready. I don't talk from a podium, but I have a little music stand right on the side where I have a couple of notes, and it's where my runners will put post-it notes for me.

Then I take a little sip of water and take my three deep breaths. One...two...three...to center myself. I wait to hear my name. "Ladies and gentlemen, author of The Power to Speak Naked, Sean Tyler Foley." Then I walk on the stage, focused on getting to my mark.

Then with my final part of the pre-talk routine, as I scan the audience, I take a moment to look, and I try to find at least three faces that I like. They're my people. Some people in the audience will 'speak' to you—they have a special energy. Those three people are going to be my anchor through the rest of the talk. Once I've found them, then I launch into my presentation. That's my routine.

Other Ideas to Ground Yourself

One other suggestion I would make is that you find something that you can do to ground yourself within the first ten seconds of your talk. For example, Tony Robbins slaps his hand and yells, "boom", so people know he is ready to go. If he is jittery, or nervous, this is his way of grounding himself when he starts.

In addition, I know a couple of people who squeeze their hand behind their back, and they make a fist, then they count to three and start their talk. I also know someone who stands in the Superman pose for a few minutes right before they start to speak. And finally, one of my coaching clients who is a phenomenal speaker, Jenn Traxel, takes two steps forward before she speaks.

For her, that means she is stepping into her greatness, and that is a great way to center yourself before beginning the presentation. Whatever you decide to do before you start speaking, find something that grounds you. Make sure it calms your nerves and embodies who you are.

Having a pre-talk routine is so important because it is the compilation of everything you do to prepare before you begin your presentation. All world-class performers, whether they are speakers, singers, athletes, or anyone else, have a pre- performance routine that centers them, calms them down, and directs their energy in a constructive manner so that they can deliver the value they are planning to provide. The tips provided here are suggestions for guidance. Take what works for you, or even adapt your routine based on what you have read, and then discard the rest. If you believe you would benefit from a personal coaching session, I would be happy to explore that with you.

Key Takeaways: ——————————————

- Having a specific pre-talk routine that you can rely on is important. It will calm your nerves and get you ready to be your very best onstage.

- If possible, meet some of your audience members before your talk. Use F.O.R.D. when speaking to them (Family, Occupation, Recreation, Dreams).

- Do vocal warm-ups before your presentation. It prepares your voice so you can project and enunciate clearly during your talk.

What Is Your Big Why?

In my work, I encounter people who want to become full-time public speakers or others who don't love speaking but know they have to be good at it for the sake of their careers. There is nothing wrong with either one of these, but knowing your big why is critical because when things get rough—and they do for all of us—will help you keep going when you don't feel enthusiastic.

We all have goals, but it's important to ask why. Why do you want to become a public speaker? Why do you want to have a healthier lifestyle? Why do you want the promotion at work?

You might have some canned answers for those questions, but what is your real why? It's important to dig deep and discover your real source behind your motivation so that you can continue to strive toward that goal when you don't want to. A strong why will propel you forward.

A more concrete why may be less obvious than surface reasons, but it creates powerful motivation to pursue the goal you are going after, and it will give you a sense of purpose and accomplishment. It's intrinsic motivation. It's the thing that propels you forward as opposed to a superficial why such as wanting to own a car or wanting to look good.

Therefore, it's important to drill down until you find the reason that makes you move.

To illustrate, I will use what I call The Mackenzie Principle. Mackenzie is my three-year-old daughter, and she is constantly asking me, "Why?" and "Why, Daddy?" In fact, she won't stop asking until I have satiated her curiosity.

Grab a pen and paper because I have a written exercise for you to do.

Start by clearly stating your objective and writing it down. Let's say that your goal is to become a speaker. Ask yourself, "Why?" Your answer might be that you love the stage.

Ask, "Why?" again. Your answer might be that you want to gain more authority in your field.

Ask, "Why?" again. Consider what might be different for you if you were perceived as an authority. Your income could be higher because you could get a raise from your boss or charge more money for your consulting services.

Whatever your reasons are, you want to keep writing them down. Keep asking "Why?" as you write. You might ask this a few times or many times depending on how quickly you can drill down to your ultimate reason for accomplishing your goal.

Keep asking until—like Mackenzie—you can't possibly ask any more questions. Take time with this exercise and be patient with it. When you find it, hang on to that why. Tape it somewhere visible and use it as a constant reminder to yourself about why you want to reach your goal.

When you start to feel your motivation wane or you start to struggle with your results, return to your written statement. Remember why you have to pursue your goal no matter what.

Here's another way to think about your big why. Let's say that my daughter is across the room from me. If I laid a rope down on the ground, I could walk across it easily and get her because there is no danger. Even if the rope was elevated twelve inches above the ground, I could still walk across it without a second thought. Let's raise the bar. If that rope was stretched across two towers that were one-hundred stories high, I might not be so eager to make that trip. But if the building that my daughter was in was on fire...

I would absolutely walk across the rope to the other side no matter how high it was off the ground—because she is my big why.

Asking yourself why is so important. What would make you walk off of a perfectly stable platform and onto a rickety wire one-hundred stories above the ground? What is the motivation that would make you do that? What is the reason you would wake up in the morning and pursue your goal no matter what the obstacles are?

Drill down and ask yourself, "Why?" until you get to your ultimate reason for pursuing and achieving what you want.

As this relates to speaking, remember there will be sacrifices you will make to achieve what you want.

When we watch and listen to speakers, we usually see only the glamorous part where that person stands on stage and delivers their talk. What we don't often see is the sacrifice that often happens for that person to reach the stage.

We discussed the preparation, the planning, and all the work that goes into doing the talk.

Many times, the speaker is talking at someone else's event. However, there are times when that speaker puts on the event themselves. On one such occasion, I was doing a talk on publishing success. My job was to fill the room and to deliver value to as many people as possible. after spending $800 on the combination of Facebook ads and the cost of the venue, I had exactly four people in the audience.

Four.

I gave that talk as if I had one-hundred people in the audience. My game face was on, and I gave a terrific speech.

It was tough to do that talk with the same energy that I always bring, but I did it anyway. When the talk was over, all four people said they got value from it. Of course, that made me glad.

But the real win was when I saw my wife and little girl in the back of the room as I was finishing. I do this so I can provide for them. No matter how large or small my audience is, my goal is to provide value to those who hear me and make enough money to give them a lifestyle they deserve.

For me, it all comes down to family.

One More Thing About my Big Why

I lost my father at a very early age, so I know the importance of telling your story before it's too late. I know the impact of a story not told. That is the driving factor behind everything that I do with public speaking and Total Buy In. I want to empower everyone to tell their story before they don't have the chance to do it.

As you progress through your speaking journey, I am confident that when you define your big reason why, it will carry you through the good times and the bad—and there will be both. Speaking is a great way to impact lives and make a living.

If this is something you aspire to, I would love to continue this conversation with you. Go to seantylerfoley.com or use the QR code to learn more about what I do and how I can help you on this journey.

Scan me

It would be my honor to do so.

Key Takeaways:

- You need to discover the ultimate reason why you're are doing something, or you won't follow through when things get difficult.

- Remember The Mackenzie Principle. What cause would make you walk across a wire between two buildings one-hundred stories above the ground? That's your Mackenzie.

- Anything worth having is not as glamorous as it may seem. There will be sacrifices to be made in the pursuit of your goals. Average people will let those obstacles stop them, but you are not one of them. Find your ultimate why and your chances of success will be much higher.

It's A Wrap, Folks

By now, you should have a pretty good idea about what goes into preparing and delivering a great presentation. Be sure to review this book as often as necessary because you will likely get something different out of it every time. In a sense, it's like watching a movie that you enjoy over and over again—it's quite common to find something new that you missed the first time around.

We talked about a lot of important concepts: planning, preparing, discovering who your audience is, harnessing nervous energy in a constructive manner, being authentically you, finding your voice, having a pre-talk routine, and much more.

One more idea I want to briefly address. Part of your pre-talk visualization can also include the feeling you have when you finish and imagining the reaction from your audience.

How did your audience receive your talk?

How did you feel when it was done?

Imagine the impact you can have on audiences all over your community, your state or province, your country, or even worldwide. It's a rush that won't go away.

In fact, the feeling you get when you crush your presentation is indescribable. Believe it or not, I am an introvert, which is the opposite of what you might imagine. However, being on stage and impacting many people at once, taking them on an emotional journey that I designed, and getting them to laugh, cry, or think when I want them to is all very powerful and life-changing, not only for them but also for me. The energy exchange that happens in a speaking situation can be very exciting, especially when the message is well-executed, and the audience is fully engaged. It's the greatest drug on the planet because it's a natural high and you have changed peoples' lives. When you have delivered a talk that comes from authenticity and honesty, and it is delivered from a place of love, it's better than chocolate, it's better than sex, and it's the greatest feeling ever.

For those who doubt that last statement, when is the last time you received applause after sex?

Seriously.

Once you get used to speaking in front of others, it can become a bit addicting—but in a good way.

As I mentioned at the very beginning of the book, I believe that if you are living and breathing, then you have a powerful message inside you that needs to be heard.

The world deserves to hear that message, and it needs to come from you.

You have the power to speak your truth; you have the power to speak your message, and now...

You have The Power to Speak Naked.

About the Author

Sean Tyler Foley is the managing director of Total Buy In, an organization designed to help speakers find their voice and get on stages to share their message.

He has been performing and speaking publicly ever since his first Christmas play at the age of six. After that first time he kept an audience entertained, he knew that he had that gift and passion for the power of performance and captivating those who watch.

For Sean Tyler, there's a magic that comes through the room when you make an entire auditorium feel any emotions. The audience goes through that shared experience with you, but you control it and take them on the journey.

His love of performing has also spread to film, television, and stage projects. These include appearances in *Freddy vs. Jason*, *Door to Door*, *Carrie*, and the musical *Rag Time*.

In addition to his speaking career, Sean Tyler is also a serial entrepreneur running multiple businesses, and has run for political office.

To learn more about the Sean Tyler Foley and his services, go to seantylerfoley.com.

Bridging The Gap Between Marketing & Sales

Many businesses have trouble:

- ✓ Offering quality customer service
- ✓ Eliminating inefficiencies
- ✓ Scaling their business
- ✓ Handling more leads

Is this you? No worries!

We build SYSTEMS that help FIX this & MORE!

Protecting
your *Interests*
Locally & Globally

silklegal.com

I WILL HELP YOU WRITE YOUR BOOK!

Many people dream of writing a book someday, but most of them never get around to doing it. Why not?

- You hadn't thought about it before
- You don't think you have time or know how
- You might not believe you are a good enough writer

When you are working with an experienced coach, these reasons go away because I will help you every step of the way. As a published author, I can tell you that having a book of your own is critical to growing your business.

Here are some great reasons to have a book:

— Added credibility because people automatically give expert status to those who have written a book.

— Stand out against your competitors who do NOT have a book. Telling your prospect, "Here is a book that answers many of the common questions you might have about...." could help generate more leads and sales.

— Extra sources of revenue, and not just with book sales! Obtain new customers and referrals, speaking opportunities, TV/radio interviews, and talks in your local community which could lead to attracting new customers.

As a published author of several books, I can help you put this all together. Visit **www.briankwright.com** or email me at **brian@briankwright.com** to begin the discussion.